Online Conferences

*Professional Development
for a Networked Era*

**Lynn Anderson
Terry Anderson**

T0344505

INFORMATION AGE PUBLISHING, INC.
Charlotte, NC • www.infoagepub.com

Library of Congress Cataloging-in-Publication Data

Anderson, Lynn.
  Online conferences : professional development for a networked era / Lynn
Anderson, Terry Anderson.
      p. cm.
  Includes bibliographical references.
  ISBN 978-1-61735-138-9 (pbk.) – ISBN 978-1-61735-139-6 (hardcover) –
ISBN 978-1-61735-140-2 (e-book)
1. Professional education–Congresses. 2. Continuing
education–Congresses. 3. Computer conferencing. I. Anderson, Terry, 1950-
II. Title.
  LC1072.C56A53 2010
  378'.0130285478–dc22

                                                              2010041400

Contents

Introduction ix

1 Continuing Professional Education: An Historical Overview 1

Introduction 1

History 2

Definition, Goals, and Reality.. 2

CPE Conferences 3

The Conference Industry.. 5

Barriers to Participation... 5

Trends in CPE 6

   Lifelong Learning... 6

   Constructivist and Connectivist Learning Models........................ 7

   Communities of Practice.. 9

   Distance Education (e-Learning).. 10

Conclusion... 11

2 What is an Online CPE Conference?....................................... 13

Introduction 13

What Is an Online Conference? 14

The Evolution of Online Conferencing 15

   First Generation: Text-Based Asynchronous............................... 16

   Generation Two: Real Time... 18

   Generation Three: Immersion.. 19

Advantages of Online Conferences... 21

Disadvantages of Online Conferences 25

Conclusion... 25

3 Technologies: From Text to Immersion 27

    Introduction 27

    The Conference Platform 28

    The Mashup 31

    One-Way Media Used to Present Content 32

    Asynchronous Technologies 33

        Email 33

        Text Messaging (SMS) 36

        Bulletin Boards/Forums 36

        Web 2.0 Technologies 37

    Synchronous Technologies 39

        Live Text Chat (Instant Messaging) 40

        Live Web Conferencing 40

        Video 41

        Multi-User Virtual Environments: Second Life 42

    Looking to the Future 44

    Conclusion 46

4 Synchronous versus Asynchronous Conferencing Technologies 47

    Introduction 47

    Synchronous Conferencing 48

        Disadvantages 48

    Asynchronous Conferencing 50

        Temporal Flexibility 50

        Lack of Physical Presence 52

    Conclusion 53

5 Conference Components, Formats, and Design 55

    Introduction 55

    Components of Typical Online CPE Conferences 56

    Organizational Models 58

        Case Study 60

    Dual-Mode Conferences 63

        Case Study of a Dual-Mode Conference: 64

    Emerging Trends 65

        Unconferences 65

Design Considerations 67

    Participant Characteristics 68

Organizational Factors 70

Conclusion 71

6 Online Conference Evaluation 73

Introduction 73

Evaluation Theory 74

Current Evaluation Practices 75

New Evaluation Methods 78

    Responsive Evaluation in an Online Professional Conference 80

    New Learning 82

    New Learning in an Online Professional Conference 84

Conclusion 84

7 Emergence of Infrastructure and Commercial Support
for Online Conferences 87

Introduction 87

Commercial Support for the Organization and Delivery of
Online Conferences 88

    The Consultants-E 89

    Direct Learn Online Conferencing 91

    iCohere 93

    LearningTimes 96

    ON24 and Unisfair 97

Conclusion 99

8 Organizer Perspectives 101

Introduction 101

Interview Method 102

    The Interview Questions 102

    Analysis & Synthesis 103

Common Themes from Experienced Online Conference
Organizers 104

    Commercial Sponsors 105

    Promoting the Online Conference 105

    Call for Papers/Presentations 106

Flexibility Afforded Conference Organizers...................................... 107

Participation: The Unknown Factor... 108

Making the Delegates Comfortable and Encouraging Interaction..111

Promoting Attendance and Participation during the Conference . 112

Live Presentations 113

Supporting Presenters... 113

Presenter Freedom to Choose Media 114

*Encouraging Interaction and Networking (Building a
Community)*...116

Dealing with a Global Audience 118

Perceived Benefits of Online Conferences...................................119

Conclusion.. 120

9 Summary of Best Practices and Making Change Happen 121

Introduction 121

Summary of Best Practices... 122

Making Change Happen... 126

Supporting and Championing Innovation 127

Conclusion.. 130

References... 131

Introduction

Networked information and communication technologies have revolutionized business, communication, entertainment, and the social lives of most citizens of the world. We have entered an era of pervasive networking. These networks afford informational retrieval, multiple forms of low cost communication, and the capacity to share and grow knowledge among people scattered around the world as well as among those sitting in the office next door. All of this change creates both opportunity and pressure on existing practices, businesses, and institutions. These changes may be sustaining, in that the use of networked technologies allows existing business or service models to continue while taking advantage of incremental improvements or cost reductions to enhance services or profits. Conversely, the network technologies may be disruptive, challenging existing business models and creating opportunities for new competitors to radically affect current practice.

In this text we focus on the online evolution of the venerable tradition of face-to-face gathering of professionals that defines the continuing professional education conference—a scheduled and formal opportunity for people sharing common interest or vocation to confer with each other. Though varying by tradition, business culture, and discipline, a professional conference usually consists of formal and scheduled talks and presentations by celebrity keynotes. These are usually followed by smaller sessions where members of the organization are invited to share insights, developments, concerns, and issues in panel or individual presentations. Often the conference and its audience attract businesses wishing to sell specialized products to the delegates, and these form a tradeshow at which vendors display and promote their wares.

Online Conferences: Professional Development for a Networked Era, pages ix–xiv
Copyright © 2010 by Information Age Publishing
All rights of reproduction in any form reserved.

Arguably the most important function of the conference (and especially important in the context of the arguments presented in this text) is the creation of opportunities for informal socialization, entertainment, and networking. This informal component of the conference creates opportunities for deal making, developing of social capital, sharing of insider knowledge and news, and bonding and friendship building by members of that community. These social activities are typically "lubricated" by food and drink and often professional entertainment designed to help members relax and enjoy each others' company.

Networked technologies are proving disruptive to this model of professional development. These disruptions originate from two opposite directions. Most important, and the subject of this text, is the capacity for professional groups to organize online conferences that do not require participants to physically travel to a central gathering place. Online conferences are being held regularly, some mimicking their place-bound predecessors with well-known keynote presenters, break out rooms, forums for presentation and discussion, virtual tradeshows, and opportunities for informal socialization and entertainment. Others are offering radical new forms of conferencing using both synchronous (in real time) and asynchronous opportunities to confer that leave permanent records in multi-media formats. Each of these technologies and the activities designed to exploit their affordances are described in detail in later chapters.

Networked technologies are also invading face-to face conferences. As often as not, delegates now multi-task at conferences with a laptop computer or other portable device open during sessions. Some of this attention is functioning as a distraction as the activities and concerns of home intrude into the attention of the conference attendee. But increasingly, participants are using Twitter, blogs, and other networking tools to comment upon, record for others, or rebroadcast ideas presented in the sessions. Increasingly, conference organizers are web-casting keynote talks as they happen, opening the session to a new global audience, some of whom annotate and contribute to a communication *back channel* with comments and questions. The networks thus serve even the traditional face-to-face conference by providing a back channel for those in attendance and, increasingly, for those following the conference at a distance.

The benefits and capabilities of online conferences are increasing at network speed. Conference organizers can choose among many tools to create the online conference environment that takes advantage of both synchronous activities that engage audiences and asynchronous discussions that allow participants from different time zones around the world and those with time constraints to participate at their convenience. Obviously, the travel, accommodation, and restaurant charges for organizers, participants, and presenters are completely eliminated by the online conference. This reduction comes at a time when these costs are rising and most organizational training budgets are shrinking. Perhaps of even greater benefit is the huge reduction in the greenhouse gas emissions that are associated with both hosting and travelling to and from face-to-face conferences. Finally, the opportunity costs associated with time lost in travel, disruption to the work place and home, and the personal costs to families and social organizations due to participation in face-to-face conferences are large. At the same time as the potential benefits of online conferences are increasing, the costs of face-to-face conferences are increasing. This combination of costs and technological change presents both challenge and opportunities for conference organizers.

This text is designed to provide guidance and advice to those wishing to design and deliver online professional development conferences. We examine the theoretical models of effective professional development, the components of effective continuing professional education, the affordances of networking technologies, and lessons learned by successful online conference organizers. The text describes various ways in which networking technologies are being used to support successful online professional development events. Resources for conference organizers are given in the form of links to commercial and open source software as well as information about companies providing platforms and comprehensive support for the organization of online conferences. Finally, a list of best practices based on the research literature, experiences of the authors, and interviews with experienced online conference organizers is presented in the final chapter. A brief summary of the chapter contents is provided here.

Chapter 1: Continuing Professional Education: An Historical Overview

This chapter looks at the development of continuing professional education (CPE) as a general area of study, focusing on the goals of CPE and the delivery methods used to achieve these goals. Formal CPE events, specifically face-to-face conferences, are discussed in light of their effectiveness and accessibility. For example, traditional face-to-face conferences have been criticized for relying on presenter-led sessions that are ineffective and uninspiring. Further, face-to-face conferences pose accessibility issues, due to the cost and time required to attend. The chapter closes with a look at the trends evident in the literature on professional development:

- The promotion of lifelong learning
- The adoption of constructivist and connectivist learning models
- Communities of Practice
- Distance Education (e-Learning)

E-learning is presented as a means of addressing accessibility issues while at the same time offering a platform that may be utilized to advance the other trends.

Chapter 2: Literature Review of Online CPE Conferencing

This chapter describes and defines the characteristics of online CPE conferences. It then reviews the history of online conferences, focusing on the evolution through three generations of technology: asynchronous, synchronous, and immersive environments. The remainder of the chapter looks at the advantages and disadvantages of online conferences in comparison to traditional face-to-face conferences.

Chapter 3: Technologies: From Text to Immersion

In this chapter, we describe the technological tools available to conference organizers and the various ways they may be integrated or "mashed up" for the purpose of an online professional conference. Examples of how these technologies have been employed in online CPE conferences are provided. The chapter is organized into four sections:

- Online Conferencing Platforms
- One-way Presentation Media
- Asynchronous Interactive Technologies, including Web 2.0
- Synchronous Interactive Technologies, including MUVEs

To assist in the selection of conferencing software, we have included a list of Web sites that provide names, links, and evaluations of commercial and open-source conferencing software at the end of the chapter.

Chapter 4: Synchronous vs. Asynchronous Conferencing Technologies

This chapter compares the advantages and disadvantages of synchronous and asynchronous conferencing technologies. For example, synchronous technologies have been credited with providing "a sense of immediacy and spontaneity" (Anderson, 1996) as well as a higher level of social presence

compared to asynchronous conferencing. However, synchronous conferencing technologies require that dispersed participants be "present" at the
same time. This restrictive characteristic of synchronous events presents
a barrier to participation, particularly for participants from various time
zones. Although asynchronous technologies do not offer the same level of
social presence, they provide temporal flexibility to participants and support more reflective and considered participation. An understanding of the
unique capabilities of each form of interaction, allows online conference
organizers to create appropriate blends and mixes that match the need of
their presenters and target audiences.

Chapter 5: Conference Components, Formats, and Design

This chapter looks at the activities that are often included within an online
conference and the organizational formats that are possible. For example,
an online conference can include many of the same components as a traditional face-to-face conference (e.g., registration, social events, keynote
addresses, exhibition halls, etc.). In addition, online conferences can offer interactive spaces that allow dispersed participants to collaborate, share
conference-related content, and network long after the formal conference
events have ended.

Online conferences support a wide variety of organizational models.
Conference organizers may choose to hold the conference completely online or to offer a dual-mode conference in which the online portion expands the reach of a traditional face-to-face conference. Various formats
currently in use are described and analyzed in terms of the interaction supported by the model and the flexibility afforded to participants. Finally, this
chapter examines the factors that influence design decisions.

Chapter 6: Online Conference Evaluation

The evaluation of conferences is often treated as an afterthought, involving
little more than a questionnaire distributed after conference proceedings.
These often result in low return rates and little valuable information. The
source of this problem may be seen in the lack of incentives and scholarly
attention given to the evaluation of professional conferences. This chapter
provides a brief review of evaluation theory, examines the limitations of current evaluation practices, describes emerging models, and discusses how
these models may be implemented within an online CPE conference.

Chapter 7: Emergence of Infrastructure and Commercial Support for Online Conferences

This chapter looks at several companies that are now offering comprehensive services for both the organization and delivery of online CPE conferences. These companies provide expertise to corporations, organizations, and associations who would like to host a CPE event online but lack the experience and know-how necessary to make the event successful. Information on these companies was obtained directly from their Web sites, promotional material, and interviews with company executives. This examination is intended to raise awareness of the software and services available to organizations wishing to host an online conference. Links to company Web sites are provided in a table at the end of the chapter.

Chapter 8: Organizer Perspectives

In order to learn more about the evolution of online conferences, current activities, and best practices, we sought out and interviewed over a dozen online conference organizers. These conference organizers were selected because of their experience planning, coordinating, and facilitating multiple online conferences over several years. The conferences produced by the interviewees varied in length, number of presentations, media, and organization. Despite the variation in the conferences organized, some commonalities appeared. In this chapter, we pull together some of the common themes that emerged from the interviews in order to shed light on the lessons learned and current practices of experienced online conference organizers.

Chapter 9: Summary of Best Practices and Making Change Happen

This closing chapter provides a brief summary of the common themes and best practices that emerged from our study. In addition, the latter part of the chapter addresses the issue of organizational change and the obstacles that may be faced by conference organizers wishing to make the move to online conferences. Strategies to encourage change and acceptance of online professional conferences are provided.

1

Continuing Professional Education

An Historical Overview

Introduction

Much of this text examines the ways in which networked technologies are changing professional education conferences. However, it is important that we not lose focus on the purpose of these conferences while discussing the media used for their support. Continuing professional education (CPE) serves a vital role in today's society. Rapid social changes, improved research-based knowledge, and increasing technological innovations require professionals to constantly update their skills and knowledge in order to remain relevant and effective. This chapter looks at the development of CPE as a general area of study, focusing on the goals of CPE and the delivery methods used to achieve these goals. Formal CPE events, specifically face-to-face conferences, are discussed in light of their effectiveness and accessibility. Finally, the chapter closes with a look at the most pervasive trend in CPE—the move toward online distance education.

Online Conferences: Professional Development for a Networked Era, pages 1–11
Copyright © 2010 by Information Age Publishing

History

Continuing professional education (CPE), as a general area of study, is still relatively young, experiencing the growth and change typical of youth. Professionalization, with incumbent responsibilities for quality control, adherence to ethical standards, and proficiency has been a component and a goal of many white- and blue-collar workers. Most professionals realize that training and development must be continuous if they are to remain competent and capable of working effectively throughout their working careers; thus, the need for both formal and informal opportunities to participate in CPE. Most literature on CPE associates the infancy of this area of study with the 1980s. Beginning with Houle's seminal book, *Continuing Learning in the Professions* (1980), "the decade witnessed a stream of books and high level proposals from many professions seeking to improve the ways that continuing education is conceptualized, organized and delivered" (Cervero, 2001, p. 17). This sudden "stream" of literature is credited to the rise in the number of professions that occurred in the 1960s and '70s. As the number of professions increased, so too did the public's dependency on these professions. This dependency led to growing concern over professional obsolescence and accountability (Azzaretto, 1990). *Professional obsolescence* is defined as the "discrepancy between a professional's body of knowledge, skills and abilities and the individual's capability to perform the required tasks at hand as well as those planned for the future" (Dublin, 1990, p. 10). "Beginning in the 1960s, the public perception of professional responsibility, accountability, and service was challenged by clients and consumers of these services and government agencies, leading to a climate of litigation across the professions" (Cervero, 2001, 23). Professional associations responded to these concerns with greater emphasis on standards of performance, continuing education, re-licensure, and re-certification processes (Cervero & Azzareto, 1990; Mott, 2000). The public's expectations of professionals were expressed with increasing regularity. Freidson (1983) noted that "The professions 'strike a bargain with society' in which they exchange competence and integrity against the trust of client and community, relative freedom from lay supervision and interference, protection against unqualified competition as well as substantial remuneration and higher social status" (p. 41). Therefore, it was and is seen as both an ethical and professional obligation of those in the professions to remain current in their chosen field of expertise.

Definition, Goals, and Reality

In the U.S., the number of states requiring continuing education for re-licensure has risen consistently since the 1980s (Cervero, 2001). However, research on CPE as a general area of study remains limited. The research that does exist tends to be related to specific professions. This is also true of the name by which CPE is known. "Specific terms are used in some professions to refer to the same type of activity; lawyers speak of continuing legal education (CLE); doctors of continuing medical education (CME); and engineers—simply of continuing education (CE)" (Brennan, 1990, p. 8). In addition, the word *development* is often used rather than *education*. That said, the definition of CPE (if not the name) is fairly consistent across the professions. Most of the literature defines CPE as the education and training of professionals beyond their initial pre-service training and induction of licensing into professional practice (Brennan, 1990; Houle, 1980; Meyer, 2007). Formal CPE is often differentiated from informal CPE for the purpose of licensure and research. Formal CPE activities are usually seen as those that are institutionally sponsored, classroom-based, or highly structured (Marsick & Watkins, 2001). Formal CPE activities include, but are not limited to, university courses, conferences, workshops, seminars, and certificate programs (Smith et al., 2006). Informal activities are those that are less structured, self directed, and involve networking, coaching, and mentoring (Marsick & Watkins, 2001). Peer consultation, reading journals and books, networking events, and mentoring are all considered informal CPE activities.

The goal of CPE is also fairly consistent across the professions. It has been described generally as the establishment, maintenance, and improvement of professional knowledge, skills, and attitude resulting in improved performance (Cervero, 2001; Knox, 2000; Mott, 2000). However, a consensus on the best means through which this goal is to be realized has not yet emerged. Cervero (2001) describes the existing systems of continuing education as "primitive." Most are characterized as "devoted mainly to updating practitioners about the newest developments, which are transmitted in a didactic fashion and offered by a pluralistic group of providers (workplaces, for-profit agencies, and universities) that do not work together in any co-ordinated fashion" (2001, p. 18). It is our hope that the persistence, transparency, and visibility of online activities will lead to increased coordination amongst these disparate groups. In addition, we believe that the emerging pedagogies associated with online learning will evolve new patterns and means of CPE that prove more effective and more efficient.

CPE Conferences

Cervero's "updating" depiction of continuing education systems aptly describes the traditional CPE conference. It is, typically, a three- to four-day gathering of professionals at a central venue, commencing with a social activity, and followed by multiple PowerPoint presentations from various experts in the field. Conference participants sit listening for hours upon hours with little time given for questions or discussion. The proceedings are dominated by the "informational update" (Nowlen, 1988). The learning theory implied by the traditional conference is the transfer model, which assumes that minds are empty vessels waiting to be filled. However, as Ravn (2007, p. 215) points out, "textbooks on educational theory and practice paint pictures of learning and knowledge creation that are pretty much the exact opposite of the professional conference."

Despite this bleak description, each year, millions of professionals take time away from their work and families in order to attend these costly events. The popularity of CPE conferences can be attributed to several factors. First, regulatory bodies struggling to develop accountability mechanisms have utilized participation in formal CPE events as the method of choice. Learning and competence are equated with the number of courses and conferences attended (Meyer, 2007). However, these requirements have been critiqued for promoting "the appearance of accountability but [have done] little or nothing to address the underlying issue of competence" (Queeney, 2000, p. 378), and of greater concern is that there is often little impact of the development on continuing practice. Second, traditional conferences provide an opportunity for professionals with similar interests to meet and interact, if not during the formal sessions, then between and after events. This social networking, in real time, is valued by both participants and employers as a way to add informal learning and professional networking to formal conference activities. Third, travel to a traditional conference provides professionals with an opportunity to escape the demands of their jobs in order to focus on learning and networking with the hopes of being inspired. Finally, CPE conferences are often hosted in exciting and exotic locales, thereby offering professionals a chance to experience new places and build in leisure time or tourist activities.

These simultaneous advantages and disadvantages of professional conferences were aptly illustrated when the second author was interviewing medical doctors on their attitudes towards professional development in small towns in Northern Ontario. When queried about the major disadvantages of the prevalent CPE model within the medical community—attendance at professional conferences in large (but distance) cities—doctors cited the problems associated with travel and absence from home and workplace. Ironically, when queried about the advantages associated with this type of CPE, they responded with the same issues, only expressed as the advantages of being able to travel and get away from home and workplace responsibilities. This dichotomist reaction, felt by many, suggests that the face-to-face conference will not be completely displaced by online conferences. Just as movies did not completely eliminate live theater, nor television replace movies, the online conference has emerged as a cost- and time-effective alternative that will allow substitution and greater accessibility, but will likely not eliminate the rich social experience and travel opportunities associated with face-to-face conferences

The Conference Industry

In the 1980s and '90s, the demand for formal CPE events resulted in an explosion in both the professional education industry and the meeting and event industry. Until recently, the provision of CPE conferences continued to rise (Daley, 2001; MPI, 2009). However, the harsh realities of the 2008 economic downturn have forced many professionals and their employers to rethink their spending. Surveys conducted by meeting industry experts early in 2009 predicted that attendance at professional conferences would reach a plateau (ICCA, 2009; MPI, 2009).

Despite the reported growth and size of the meeting and event industry, there is very little hard data available on the economic impact of professional conferences worldwide. A recent survey of member activities released by the International Association of Professional Conference Organizers (IAPCO) provides only a glimpse of the revenue generated by this industry. The IAPCO is a relatively small organization representing only 100 professional conference organizer (PCO) companies worldwide (not including the U.S.); yet, according to the survey results, its members organized in excess of 5000 events in 2008, representing some 1.96 million delegates. The report estimated the economic impact to be in the region of 3.18 billion Euros ($4.64 billion USD) based on the average delegate spending 1620 Euros (IAPCO, 2009). Unfortunately, it is not clear what proportion of these events were specifically CPE events. More importantly, there is very little data on either the impact of these events on the development of professional skills or knowledge or the impact (if any) on this skill acquisition on practice (Furze & Pearcey, 1999; Meyer, 2007).

Barriers to Participation

Although the provision of CPE conferences has risen, accessibility to these events is problematic for many professionals. There exist a number of barriers, in addition to the financial restraints imposed by the economic downturn, to participation in CPE conferences. A great deal of the literature concerning these barriers is focused on the issues faced by health care professionals in particular. However, these obstacles are not unique to this field. A common theme in the literature is the problem posed by geographic distance and the associated costs of providing CPE to health professionals across dispersed communities. These costs include the financial costs of travel, work time lost, and the personal cost of time away from family. In addition, many rural health care professionals are "the sole providers of health care in their communities [and] simply cannot leave to attend an educational session, regardless of how beneficial it might be for their patients and their practices" (Curran, Fleet, & Kirby, 2006, p. 51). Nurses in particular seem to experience specific challenges in accessing CPE. Difficulty in obtaining study leave, low staffing levels, lack of support from managers, insufficient or late information about CPE events, and the lack of funding have been cited as the most common obstacles for nurses to the uptake of CPE (Barriball & While, 1996; Furze & Pearcey, 1999). In particular, enrolled nurses, part-time nurses, and those working night duty have considerable fewer opportunities to attend CPE programs than full-time or day-duty nurses.

Trends in CPE

Many of the trends prevalent in the literature and witnessed in practice address the issues of CPE effectiveness and accessibility. These trends cover several distinct themes:

- ▪ The promotion of lifelong learning
- ▪ The adoption of constructivist and connectivist learning models
- ▪ Communities of practice
- ▪ Distance education (e-Learning)

Lifelong Learning

Much of the current literature makes the argument that CPE should not be considered a separate stage of education, but rather be a part of the process of lifelong learning (Knox, 2000; Mott, 2000). According to Houle (1980), "The needs of society require that every profession become better than it is, and at least part of the effort it must exert is the improvement of its patterns of lifelong learning" (p. 30). Houle further argues that "much of every professional's attitude toward future learning and the ability to undertake it has been established by the time of entry into service" (p. 90). This sentiment has been echoed by Livneh and Livneh (1999), who suggested that pre-service training programs should incorporate CPE into the curriculum. In this way, "new professionals not only develop skills of lifelong independent learning but also begin a habit of engaging in CPE activities as practitioners who believe in and will continue their professional development" (Mott, 2000, p. 102). Unfortunately, the predominant model of pre-service education is face-to-face education in campus contexts. Thus, it is not surprising that both universities and professional organizations adopt this transmission model, only delivered in smaller chunks, when they envision lifelong learning. We are, however, increasingly aware of the use of networked technologies in campus programs and the development of blended learning programs that expose pre-professionals to the benefits, pedagogies and technical requirements of learning in online contexts.

Constructivist and Connectivist Learning Models

CPE literature has recently been promoting new pedagogical approaches based on constructivist and connectivist learning models. These approaches veer away from the ineffective and often unmotivating didactic model of CPE described by Nowlen (1988) and Cervero (2001).

Principles of Constructivism

Constructivists posit that knowledge is not transmitted; rather, it is "individually constructed and socially co-constructed by learners based on their interpretations of experiences in the world" (Jonassen, Davidson, Collins, Campbell, & Bannan Haag, 1998, p. 95). According to this perspective, "learning is determined by the complex interplay among learners' existing knowledge, the social context, and the problem to be solved" (Tam, 2000, p. 52). This constructivist perspective is echoed in the CPE literature. Professionals learn, Houle (1980) maintains, through "study, apprenticeship, and experience, both by expanding their comprehension of formal disciplines and by finding new ways to use them to achieve specific ends, constantly moving forward and backward from theory to practice so that each enriches the other" (1980, p. 1). In a study of learning and professional practice, Daley (2001) investigated how knowledge became meaningful across four different professions. "Professionals across all groups in this study described how their knowledge was constantly changing and that experiences, attendance at CPE programs, and dialogue with colleagues all contributed to the continual growth and refinement of meaningful knowledge" (Daley, 2001, p. 50). Acknowledgement of the interaction of knowledge and professional practice in the learning process is repeated throughout the literature (Cervero, 1992; Daley, 2000; Mott, 2000; Schön, 1987).

Mott (2000), in a review of various models of learning and development in practice, recommends that effective CPE with the goal of developing professional expertise should be dynamic, authentic, practice-based, collaborative, and future-oriented. She expands on Cervero's (1988) argument that CPE should promote both practical knowledge and the processes by which professionals use this practical knowledge to construct an understanding of current situations of practice. "If the goal of CPE is development of professional expertise for the improvement of practice, the most effective means are practitioners' dialogue, reflection-in-action, and theory building, in which knowledge is generated from new examples, understandings, and actions, and added to already existing repertoires" (Mott, 2000, p. 30). Looking specifically at professional conferences, Ravn (2007) proposes that the goals of CPE may be better achieved at conferences that provide a forum and interaction opportunities for mutual inspiration and shared knowledge development.

Connectivist Principles of Learning

Connectivist pedagogy arises from a need to develop learning theories and activities that take advantage of the enhanced information and communication resources that are afforded by ubiquitous access to the Net. Connectivism assumes that people, information, and knowledge do not function as autonomous units, but rather each is connected by webs of context, culture, and pre-connection to others. Learning then implies the acquisition not only of facts, ideas, and concepts, but also an understanding and a placement of this content in both an individual and a connected network with other ideas and people. George Seimens (2005), who coined the term, distinguished 8 principles of connectivism:

1. Learning and knowledge rest in diversity of opinions.
2. Learning is a process of connecting specialized nodes or information sources.
3. Learning may reside in non-human appliances.
4. Capacity to know more is more critical than what is currently known.
5. Nurturing and maintaining connections is needed to facilitate continual learning.
6. Ability to see connections between fields, ideas, and concepts is a core skill.
7. Currency (accurate, up-to-date knowledge) is the intent of all connectivist learning activities.
8. Decision-making is itself a learning process. Choosing what to learn and the meaning of incoming information is seen through the lens of a shifting reality. While there is a right answer now, it may be wrong tomorrow, due to alterations in the information climate affecting the decision.

Implications for effective learning in online conferences can be deduced from these eight principles. Since learning rests in diversity, opportunity should be provided for debate and discussion and exploration of ideas in different contexts, with opportunities provided to explore diversity that emerges. Online CPE should also create and connect networks of resources that can be utilized during the conference and when the participants return to their work. The idea of learning residing in non-human appliances may seem somewhat futuristic and robot-like, but the use of machines to record, annotate, retrieve, sort, and filter information is becoming commonplace. As an example, the use of preference systems based on either implicit or explicit recommendations of others for books, music, or movies is a powerful way to use machine aggregation of collective opinion. The fifth principle implies that CPE in either face-to-face or online modes should provide ample opportunities for participants to make new acquaintances, share expertise and interest, and develop new networks with resulting increase in social capital. The sixth principle implies a need for meta-analysis of activities and for organizers to help participants draw connections between content presented across sessions. This is often done through use of summary bloggers or commentators who are skilled at such connection building. Their public dissemination of their connection building can serve as a model and a resource to participants. Online CPE is much more flexible and capable of responding very quickly to emerging issues and opportunities, and thus can be more current than often structure-bound face-to-face activities. For example, finding an emergency replacement keynote speaker for an online conference is much easier than in a face-to-face conference, as the replacement speaker does not need to worry about the cost, time, and inconveniences of unscheduled travel. Online CPE also trains participants in decision-making. Unlike in face-to-face conferences, delegates must make wise decisions about allocating their time not only to the CPE events but also to the regular encumbrances of life associated with job and family commitments. Thus, from a connectivist perspective, online CPE provides a context and opportunities not only for the acquisition of new content, but more importantly for the development of lifelong learning skills.

Communities of Practice

Following from constructivist and connectivist perspectives of professional education, communities of practice have emerged as a means of promoting "practitioners' dialogue" and consequent learning through social interaction and networking. "Communities of practice are groups of people who share a concern, a set of problems, or a passion about a topic, and who deepen their knowledge and expertise in this area by interacting on an ongoing basis" (Wenger, McDermott, & Snyder, 2002, p. 4). As Wenger (1999) points out, these communities of practice are everywhere. We all belong to communities of practice, at home, at work or school, and in our hobbies. However, the value of communities of practice in the professions and private industry has been increasingly touted in the literature pertaining to training and development (Choi, 2006; Dolezalek, 2003; Wenger, McDermott, & Snyder, 2002).

In an effort to conceptualize the professional conference, Jacobs and McFarlane (2005) derive an ideal of conferences as communities of practice where procedures of science (or research, or professional practice) are available to view and where knowledge building takes place. They propose eight functions of conferences based on this premise:

1. The formal presentation of recent developments in the field.
2. The community evaluation of those developments (both substantive and methodological).
3. The informal presentation of other relevant developments from the community (e.g., from the conference floor).
4. Discussion of the interpretations and implications of those developments.
5. Settling disagreements over these interpretations and implications.
6. Doing 1–5 according to the practical organization of a reflective community of practice.
7. Inducting inexperienced members into the community of practice by making aspects of practice explicit and therefore capable of being apprehended.
8. Ensuring that, as a whole, research and/or professional practice progresses both substantively and methodologically (p. 319).

These eight functions provide a framework for the organization of a professional conference that is based on constructivist and connectivist principles and promotes communities of practice.

Distance Education (e-Learning)

One of the most noticeable trends in CPE recently has been the increasing number of formal CPE programs being offered via distance education (Cervero, 2000, 2001; Daley, 2002; 2008 Industry Report…, 2008). Interactive online technologies have been promoted not only as a remedy for some of the barriers to CPE mentioned above, but as a means of providing more constructivist and connectivist CPE learning environments without the boundaries of distance and time (Dolezalek, 2003; Siemens, Tittenberger, & Anderson, 2008). This capacity of online technologies extends to large groups of simultaneous users. Consequently, the online environment offers a new, more accessible venue for CPE conferences. This venue provides professionals with the opportunity to learn, interact, and collaborate without having to leave their homes or offices. Like many other distance education activities, online conferences create recordable artifacts (presentations, recordings, asynchronous discussions, chats, screen captures, etc.) that allow learning to extend beyond the end of the conference. In addition, many online CPE conferences create and sustain communities of practice among professionals who are geographically dispersed, yet who are empowered to continue online interactions long after the conference has ended.

Conclusion

Continuing education is crucial to professionals wishing to stay current in an ever-changing world. However, professional education itself has been slow to evolve and adapt effective pedagogies and learning activities that address this need. Formal CPE events, professional conferences in particular, have been criticized for being ineffective, uninspiring, and inaccessible. Current literature encourages those who organize professional conferences to employ constructivist and connectivist learning approaches that are "dynamic, authentic, practice-based, collaborative, and future-oriented" (Mott, 2000). For CPE conferences, this means a radical change from the lecture dissemination approach used over the last century to one in which the conference serves as a springboard to continuous and distributed network-based learning.

Online CPE conferences offer a more accessible and cost-effective alternative to traditional face-to-face conferences. In addition, online technologies offer participants an opportunity to interact and collaborate in ways never before possible and in ways that extend long after the formal conference ends. The following chapters look at the evolution of online conferences and the potential for interactive technologies to transform the traditional CPE conference. Online conferences taking place over the past five years are examined and online conference organizers are interviewed in order to provide a description of lessons learned and a list of best practices for those wishing to organize and participate effectively in online CPE conferences.

2

What is an Online CPE Conference?

Introduction

Although attending and funding professional education events is a component of the professional lives of many and an expense line in most businesses, there is surprisingly little study of cost, learning, or practice effectiveness. The literature on continuing professional education (CPE) identifies several recurring issues regarding the effectiveness and accessibility of formal face-to-face (f2f) CPE events. These are:

- Most formal CPE events adhere to an information dissemination approach that promotes the "sage on the stage" model.
- There is little time scheduled for interaction between participants and presenters.
- Interaction between participants is pushed out to the hallways and lounges. It is not promoted within scheduled events.
- Events planned a year in advance may not offer timely information to professionals in rapidly evolving fields such as information technology (IT).

Online Conferences: Professional Development for a Networked Era, pages 13–26
Copyright © 2010 by Information Age Publishing
All rights of reproduction in any form reserved.

- Many CPE events do not provide a permanent record of the presentation or content covered.
- The cost of travel and time away from work and family create barriers to attendance.

Online education has been identified as a means of alleviating these issues. Advances in interactive online technologies now offer conference organizers a variety of platforms and software that may be used for the purpose of CPE conferences. Not only can these technologies be used to improve access to CPE, but they offer conference organizers a medium in which constructivist and connectivist learning principles may be effectively applied. Online conferencing technologies allow conference presenters and participants to share their knowledge and experiences in ways never before possible.

The online conference has, since its inception in 1992, been touted as an effective alternative to the f2f conference, but the rapidity of developments of network technologies makes discussion of the topic broad and confusing for those who are outside of the world of educational technology. Thus, the purpose of this chapter is to provide an understanding of online CPE conferences by defining the topic and describing its evolution through three generations of technology. Finally, we examine the advantages and disadvantages afforded by online professional development conferences.

What Is an Online Conference?

Despite the recent growth in the number of CPE conferences being offered online, there exists no agreed-upon definition of online conferencing. In the discourse that does exist, the terms *online conference, virtual conference, webinar,* and *Web conference* are used interchangeably to describe a wide variety of online interactions and events. Unfortunately, the phrase *Web conference* is also commonly used to describe two other technology-related activities. The term *Web conference* may be used to refer to f2f conferences that are concerned with innovations and applications of the World Wide Web. As often, the term is used to describe the type of audio, graphic, and video interaction tools used no more often than audio or videoconferencing to support groups of students or meeting participants. In order to avoid confusion, we have chosen to use the term *online conference* throughout this text. In addition, we limit the discussion of online conferences to the context of CPE. Thus, for us, an online conference is a CPE event that is organized and attended online (Anderson, 1996; Wang, 1999). A more precise definition may be derived from the characteristics attributed by Anderson (1996) to online CPE conferences:

- Online conferences are structured events comprised of one or more planned learning activities.
- The online conference is bounded within a defined period of time.
- Events may take place synchronously, asynchronously, or through a combination of synchronous and asynchronous events.
- There exists the potential for high levels of interpersonal interaction between and amongst the facilitators, presenters, and participants.

This last point is essential to the creation of a CPE event that acknowledges the relationship between knowledge and professional practice (Cervero, 1992; Schön, 1987). As Mott (2000, p. 30) argues, it is through "practitioners' dialogue, reflection-in-action, and theory building" that effective CPE will result. Consequently, the online conference is dependent upon synchronous and/or asynchronous interactive media. This final characteristic differentiates the online conference from other online CPE activities that are based solely upon one-way media such as articles, webcasts, and podcasts (Anderson, 1996). However, one-way media are often used within an online conference as a basis for discussion.

The characteristics discussed above lead us to a more concise definition for the online CPE conference:

An online conference is a structured, time delineated, professional education event that is organized and attended on the Internet by a distributed population of presenters and participants who interact synchronously and/or asynchronously by using online communication and collaboration tools.

This definition remains broad enough to include the wide variety of activities and technologies that have been, and may yet be, incorporated into online conferences. However, to better understand the current scope of these activities and technologies and their future potential, it is beneficial to look at how online conferences have evolved since their inception in 1992.

The Evolution of Online Conferencing

In less than two decades, both the technological and organizational models of online conferences have changed dramatically. These changes can be grouped within a conceptual model of online conferences in which three generations are identified:

1. Text-based asynchronous conferencing
2. Real-time conferencing
3. Immersion into virtual worlds

It should be noted that although these three generations of online conferencing are listed in the chronological order in which they originated, there has been no conclusion of any of these generations. In fact, each generation continues to evolve in parallel with the next generation, and they are often used in combination within a single online conference.

First Generation: Text-Based Asynchronous

This first-generation online conference used asynchronous text to distribute both presentation and commentary and discussion. In the first online conferences mailing lists, Usenet groups and pre-Internet networks (Fidonet, BitNet, NetNorth, etc.) were used to support presentations and subsequent discussion. These conferences were often held in conjunction with (preceding, simultaneous with, or following) a traditional face-to-face (f2f), place-bound conference. The ubiquity of text-based e-mail maximized access at a time that predated the World Wide Web and other more multimedia-intensive technologies.

The 1992 Bangkok Project (Anderson & Mason, 1993) is considered to be the first international, online conference supported on the Internet. This online conference ran as an extension of the XVI World Congress of the International Council for Distance Education (ICDE) in Bangkok, Thailand. "The Bangkok Project relied exclusively upon email and provided a series of six interactive sessions over a three week period" (Anderson, 1996, p. 123). These sessions "mirrored the f2f ICDE Congress by inviting speakers (some who were also speaking at the f2f congress) to compose opening (text-based) speeches or papers. These were followed by feedback, questions and comments from the distributed audience" (Anderson, 2005, p. 3). The technical setup of the conference was described as follows: "A central mail distribution list was established at the University of Calgary in Canada. All conference messages were posted to this central list, from which they were fed to approximately twenty-five different networks or mail discussion lists for further distribution" (Anderson & Mason, 1993, p. 6). This type of presentation-based online conference was soon replicated by a number of organizations.

By the mid-nineties, these virtual conferences began to expand into ever more sophisticated Web-based, but still asynchronous, text-based technologies. In addition, a growing number of conference organizers chose to conduct these conferences completely online. Kirkpatrick (1996) described initial usage of the Web as "limited to websites offering abstracts, schedules, preconference readings, and listservs or newsgroups for asynchronous discussions." However, it was not long before Internet service providers began offering online forums as an alternative to email. Forums enhanced the flow of conferences because, in forums, topics are organized into threads and participants can read and respond directly at relevant points in the conversation. By contrast, e-mail postings arrive chronologically and their organization is left to the individual reader, often resulting in a deluge of e-mail posts discussing a number of different topics and presentations at the same time. Thus, threaded forums were quickly adopted by conference organizers, as they provide much improved flow and discussion organization. In recent years, first generation online conferencing media has grown to include Web 2.0 technologies such as wikis, Twitter and blogs. Wikis allow participants to collaboratively edit documents (such as end-of-conference review, policy statements, etc.); blogs allow presenters (and participants) to easily compose, upload, edit, annotate, and comment upon topics raised during the online conference. Further, blogs provide a personal space that extends beyond the fixed time frame of the online conference. Though technically an asynchronous form of micro-blogging, Twitter feeds from online conferences provide a rapid sense of synchronicity to 1st generation online conferences.

Finally, before leaving this discussion of first-generation online conferences, it is worth noting that another mode of asynchronous conferencing emerged in 1999 in response to difficulties that were experienced when professionals attempted to share details of practice using only asynchronous text-based tools. Recognizing that text alone was not sufficient for the communication and learning of some complex real-world skills, Goodyear & Steeples (1999), through a European-funded project called SHARP (SHAreable Representations of Practice), developed Asynchronous Multimedia Conferencing (AMC). AMC, they claimed, enabled "knowledge that is tacit and embedded in working practices to be rendered into shareable forms for collaborative professional learning" (1999, p. 31). This was accomplished by capturing representations of practice in various video formats that were interchanged, annotated, and discussed by professionals in an asynchronous multimedia conference.

Sgouropoulou, Koutoumanos, Goodyear, and Skordalakis (2000) later extended the work begun in the SHARP project by designing a Web-based system for ordered asynchronous multimedia annotations. This system provided "an experimentation platform, for the evaluation of the pedagogical effectiveness of AMC for the sharing of working practices within a community of practitioners and learners." They endorsed the use of AMC by stating that

> it sustains most of the benefits of ATC, while at the same time it supports:
> - the efficient, low-cost creation of vivid representations of working practices (e.g. concise digitised video demonstrations and explanations by experienced practitioners),
> - the collaborative "discussion" and "critique" of these representations, over time and anywhere in space, by learners, teachers and other practitioners, using audio, video and/or textual "annotations." (Sgouropoulou et al., 2000)

This description of the first generation of largely text-based and asynchronous interaction largely parallels the technical affordance and limitations of the first-generation Internet. Asynchronous communications allowed online conferences to bridge time zones and afforded the deliberate, reflective, and editable nature of asynchronous text interaction. This generation opened many eyes to the possibility of convening professional development events at very low cost on a global scale. Yet, the limitations and lack of the kind of engagement associated with a compelling real-time presentation from a skilled keynote presenter fueled demand for a second generation of online conference.

Generation Two: Real Time

This generation added synchronous activities to online conference events. Early second-generation conferences used satellite-delivered television to allow delegates to gather at distributed, but local, sites and to participate by both watching remote activities and networking f2f with other participants at the local site. Later, more distributed, two-way tools, including audio, video, and Web conferencing tools, were used to allow participation from more sites (including home and office). As early as 1994, conference sessions for The College Conference on Composition and Communication and the Computers and Writing Conference were held on MOOs (Multi-User Dimension/Dungeon Object Oriented) to provide participants synchronous text-based interaction (Day, 1996).

In the mid-nineties, online conferencing began working its way into the mainstream with the launch of several private companies offering synchronous online conferencing software (Totty, 2005). Since that time, the rapid development of online technologies and the accessibility of large-bandwidth connections have drastically increased the number of real-time collaboration platforms available (Wang, 1999). These platforms differ in the number of features offered; however, many provide interactive white-boards, application sharing, and real-time sharing of files between present-ers and participants. Communication is facilitated through live text chats or audio interaction via a standard telephone conference call or VoIP (Voice over Internet Protocol), the transmission of audio signal over the Internet. As importantly, most of the newer Web conferencing systems allow for easy recording of presentation and text/voice interaction. These recordings can be stored and played or replayed by participants who cannot shift time or who are in time zones not compatible with the original presentation.

The first two generations of online conferencing, when used singly or together, overcome many of the technical and communications limitations associated with long-distance education. They allow for participants to see, hear, write, and otherwise communicate with each other in synchronous or asynchronous time. However, both generations tend to support a more de-tached interaction style, often time-shifted with pressing demands of home and office. It was left to the third generation of immersive technology to allow the sense of involvement and commitment associated with f2f conferences.

Generation Three: Immersion

In this current and emerging generation, real-time, multi-user virtual environments (MUVEs) are used to allow participants to attend conferences through their self-created digital characters or *avatars*. These highly graphi-cal 3-D virtual environments allow participants to move around and interact with both the environment and with other participants' avatars. MUVEs add a visual feedback element that serves to enhance the interaction between participants and provides users with a strong sense of presence (Chidress & Braswell, 2006; Cross, O'Driscoll, & Trondsen, 2007). In 1995, the Canadian Association for Distance Education (CADE) added real-time audio telecon-ferencing to their two-week, e-mail-based annual conference, while in that same year the Global Lecture Hall, held in conjunction with The Sixth In-ternational Conference on Distance Education in Cost Rica, included use of M Bone, CuSeeMe net-based video conferencing, satellite-delivered video broadcasting, and MOOs (Anderson, 1996; Wang, 1999).These environ-ments provide educators with opportunities to develop CPE activities that are dynamic, authentic, practice-based, collaborative, and future-oriented (Mott, 2000). However, as this mode of online conferencing is still in its in-fancy, literature regarding its effectiveness is extremely limited.

Although several MUVEs exist, and many more are in developmental stages, *Second Life* is considered the "poster child" of virtual worlds (Cross,

O'Driscoll, & Trondsen, 2007). *Second Life*, developed by Linden Lab, was launched on June 23, 2003. According to *Wikipedia*, by September 2008, just over 15 million accounts were registered (Second Life, 2009). However, since many users try and then do not return to *Second Life*, data indicating the number of unique users who entered *Second Life* two or more times per month is probably a more accurate reflection of the popularity of the site. In the month of May, 2009, this number peaked at 752,035 (Linden, August 2009). *Second Life* offers free resident membership; however, charges are applied for ownership of land and improved technical support. Interaction in *Second Life* is supported via local chat, global instant messaging (IM), and Voice over Internet Protocol (VoIP). Chatting and VoIP are used for localized public conversations between two or more avatars. These conversations are visible/audible to any avatar within a given distance. IM communication is private and is not dependent on proximity.

The creators of *Second Life*, Linden Labs, have been very proactive in promoting *Second Life* for educational purposes. They advertise space for educational use and boast a long list of academic institutions and organizations utilizing the *Second Life* grid. Many of these have created virtual conference centers for the purpose of CPE. In addition, private companies have established conference centers within *Second Life* where pre-designed space may be rented out for the purpose of professional education seminars and conferences (e.g., The Consultants-E SL, http://www.theconsultants-e. com/edunation/edunation.asp).

Many readers will likely have visited *Second Life* or other immersive worlds, and most become easily convinced of the fascination and engagement that comes from participation. McKerlich and Anderson (2007) investigated the sense of social presence indicators observed in immersive worlds and concluded that the environment provides much more effective clues and increased sense of presence than non-immersive online environments. However, there are technical limitations associated with demands for more powerful desktop computers and higher bandwidth that can create barriers to third-generation use. In addition, more preparation and practice is required for participation in immersive worlds. Most participants in first- and second-generation online conferences have little or no problems adapting to the technological demands of the online conference environment, as these are not unlike tools used on a daily basis by most professionals. However, setting up an account, configuring and dressing an avatar, learning how to teleport to the conference venue, and learning to talk and gesture often present large barriers to new conference-goers in third-generation venues. In addition, our own experience shows that *Second Life* is a very distracting environment (especially for novice users), and it is challenging to hold an audience's attention for any sustained period of time. Thus, each generation of online conference has advantages and related challenges, both technical and social in nature.

Advantages of Online Conferences

In spite of the fact that few formal studies of online conferencing have been published, the advantages of this new mode of professional development have been touted by both conference organizers and participants (Anderson, 1996; Kasser, 2001; Minshull, 2006; Wang, 1999). The most obvious advantage afforded by an online conference is the alleviation of travel cost and time. As Ivanoff (1998) points out, "the cost and time of travel can be a deciding factor in the attendance of a standard 'physical' conference, [whereas] a 'virtual' conference can be attended from anywhere in the world so long as the delegates have access to the appropriate equipment." This advantage of online conferences benefits not only the participants of conferences, but also their employers, "as their employees would have minimal work time loss and no travel time loss" (Anderson & Kanuka, 1997). That said, most of the literature on online conferencing asserts that, beyond the time that would have been spent travelling, online conferences should not be considered time-saving as far as the conference itself. As Minshull (2004) asserts, "an online conference is not a soft option . . . it's a real conference which demands a substantial time commitment" (p. 2). As with a f2f conference, participants must make time available to the conference if effective learning is to result (Anderson, 1996; Wang, 1999).

Other real and potential advantages of online conferences listed in the literature include:

- *Accessibility*: As mentioned in the previous chapter, lack of access to professional development (PD) conferences is an important issue for many professionals. Online conferences mitigate many of the barriers faced by professionals who work in remote areas, have children to care for, or work shifts (Anderson, 1996). In addition, the low cost and convenience of online conferences allows professionals in rapidly changing fields, such as the information and communication technologies (ICT), to attend online PD events more frequently than they would otherwise, providing them with access to timely information (Kimura & Ho, 2008). Finally, online conferences are more accessible to professionals with physical disabilities. "They are wheelchair friendly, it's easy to provide audio or text transcriptions of presentations, [and] screen readers make the discussions accessible" (Minshull, 2004, p. 2).

- *Convenience and Mobility*: In 1998, when Ivanoff asserted that an online conference could be attended from "anywhere in the world so long as the delegates have access to the appropriate equipment," he was arguing that such conferences eliminated the need for travel. However, now, with the expansion of wireless technology, not only does an online conference alleviate the need for travel, but it also enables travel. Delegates can now attend a conference from anywhere in the world as long as there is an Internet connection—in a café, a hotel, or even on a plane.

- *Greater Interaction*: It has been argued that both the quantity and quality of interaction in the formal part of an online conference can be better than that experienced in an f2f conference (Minshull, 2006; Menn, 2009). This may be attributed to several factors. First, in many online conferences, the participants are given access to material related to the conference presentation prior to the actual conference. For example, participants may be able to download the article to be discussed, a pre-recorded webcast, or a podcast in preparation for the actual conference. In this way, participants have time to consider pertinent questions they wish to ask, or they may collect further information related to the topic for sharing (Wang, 1999). Second, online conferences can be attended from anywhere in the world, thus enabling the sharing of experiences and perspectives among a global audience. Finally many types of online conferences allow for asynchronous interaction in which participants have time to carefully compose their questions or comments without pressure or competition for immediate response to a raised hand.

- *Decreased Cost*: As mentioned above, the costs associated with travel are eliminated with an online conference. However, it should also be noted that the cost savings for conference organizers are significant, as there is no longer a need to provide a physical venue or travel and accommodation costs for speakers (Anderson, 1996; Minshull, 2006) or conference organizers. These savings often translate to much reduced and even free conference registration for participants.

- *Recordings and Archives*: In most cases, online conference proceedings are recorded and saved to the conference Web site for an extended period of time. Consequently, participants can view recordings of presentations that they missed due to scheduling conflicts or time zone differences. When concurrent sessions are scheduled, participants do not have to miss a presentation when choosing to attend another taking place at the same time. They can listen to and/or view the presentation at a time convenient for them. In addition, participants can access contact information, review conference discussions, or download content shared between presenters and participants long after the conference has ended. In addition to the presentations themselves, most systems allow online discussion, questions, and other interactions with both presenter and other participants. These interactions are also normally archived and available for reading and even much later commentary and further interaction by participants

▪ *Sponsorship and Revenues*: Many online conference organizers have begun raising revenues and sponsorship for their conferences by incorporating vendor presentations. Sponsorship by vendors and the payment for participation in trade fairs are common features of f2f conferences, and there is likely to be equivalent interest by sponsors in accessing the specialized audiences attracted to online professional conferences. These presentations may be live or recorded. Interaction between the vendor and the delegates may be synchronous and/or asynchronous. In addition, some conference organizers have raised revenues by selling access to archived conference recordings or published proceedings.

▪ *Communities of Practice*: Online conferences provide an opportunity for conference organizers and participants to establish online communities of practice between participants who are separated by geographical and temporal distances (Anderson, 1996; Dolezalek, 2003; Wenger, McDermott, & Snyder, 2002). Communities of practice have been identified as a means of facilitating effective professional education (Brown & Duguid, 2000). An example of a community of practice emerging accidently from an early online conference was documented by Kirkpatrick (1996) in her chronicle of the Teaching in a Community College (TCC) Online Conference. A party to conclude the TCC Online Conference was scheduled in the "Coconut Cafe," a newly arranged lounge in the online Daedalus MOO. However, "the party at the cafe was like a beginning rather than an ending." The group continued to meet in the Coconut Cafe once a week, "discovering possibilities and applications for their own professional contacts as well as for their teaching in the near future" (Kirkpatrick, 1996).

▪ *Environmentally Friendly*: This last advantage of online conferences offers the most widespread benefit. By alleviating the need for conference organizers, presenters and participants to travel to a conference venue, the online conference significantly reduces energy consumption and the associated production of carbon dioxide (CO_2) emissions. These emissions, which make up approximately 85% of all greenhouse gases (GHG), are widely believed to contribute to climate change and the resulting ecological symptoms (Hansen, 2006; IPCC, 2007; Solomon et al., 2009).

A 2009 study of the "Supporting Deaf People (SDP), 2008" online conference, estimated that had the conference taken place in the real world, it would have generated approximately 431 metric tons of CO_2 (tCO_2) emissions (Anderson & Anderson, 2009). This online conference attracted 241 presenters and participants from 18 countries. It was assumed that had the conference taken place in the real world, it would have been held in London, England, as this city was home to the organizers and centrally located for the majority of the participants.

The method used for estimating the CO_2 emissions that would have been produced by a face-to-face (f2f) version of the SDP 2008 conference were adapted from a study done at the Norwegian Institute for Air Research (Stohl, 2008). That study estimated the CO_2 emissions associated with business travel undertaken by employees of the institute during the years 2005–2007. As in that research study, the calculations of the carbon footprint savings of the SDP Online Conference, were based on emissions caused by air travel, ground transportation and hotel use. All of the estimations and assumptions used to calculate the CO_2 emissions for this conference were chosen so that the results provided a moderate estimate of the CO_2 emissions that would have been produced by an f2f version of the SDP 2008 online conference. Other sources of emissions (e.g., related to food consumption, purchase of goods, use of conference facilities and materials, etc.) were omitted, assuming that they were either negligible or would have occurred in any case (Anderson & Anderson, 2009).

To put into perspective the magnitude of the carbon emissions that would have been generated by the SDP conference had it been held in London, the authors compared the emissions per participant to the per capita emissions of more than 200 countries around the world in 2005 (the most recent data available at the time of the study). The comparison showed that the average participant at an f2f version of the SDP 2008 conference, over the course of three days, would have produced 1.79 tCO_2—more than the average person in Brazil would have produced over the course of the entire year in 2005 (Anderson & Anderson, 2009). A comparison with more recent data shows that 1.79 tCO_2 is more than the average per capita emissions for the entire planet over the course of 2007 (CDIAC, 2010).

Disadvantages of Online Conferences

Some of the problems often associated with online conferences are the result of inappropriate use of technologies and lack of skill and experience of participants and not necessarily a characteristic of all online conferences per se. That said, two disadvantages of online conferences have been described recurrently in the literature.

The first disadvantage of the online conference is perhaps the most obvious and the most commonly cited; it is the absence of f2f informal interaction (Anderson & Kanuka, 1996; Minshull, 2004). In a review of Web-based collaborative learning, Hron & Friedrich (2003) observed that the social situations in online conferences "deviate from face-to-face situations," and, "depending on the particular communication medium, certain kinds of information (mimic, voice, gestures, clothes, etc.) are missing" (p. 71). The benefits of this social interaction and the importance of f2f communication to the purpose of CPE conferences, although difficult to quantify, seem to be valued highly by conference organizers and participants. Evidence of the value placed on f2f interaction is seen in the number of "Web conferences" that are actually f2f conferences where delegates, presumably professionals in the area of Web technologies, meet to learn about and discuss advantages of these technologies. As Sierra (2007) points out, "the people attending [these conferences] are the same people who create and evangelize the tools that make attending totally unnecessary." She has hypothesized that the missing factor in online conferences is the feeling of motivation or inspiration that is a result of the "emotional contagion" that occurs when one is surrounded by people who share the same interest and enthusiasm.

The second disadvantage relates to the lack of separation from home and work that is characteristic of a f2f conference. At a traditional conference, "there's a brick wall between you and the rest of the world" (Minshull, 2004, p. 2). However, participants in an online conference must often divide their time and attention between the competing attractions of the conference, the workplace, and the home.

The physical relocation that normally occurs during a face-to-face conference provides a spatial separation from day to day pressures and commitments. This separation can provide the face-to-face conference delegate with increased amounts of available time to absorb new information, individually reflect and socially interact, [while] the virtual conference delegate must extract time from an already limited and constrained pool. (Anderson, 1996, p. 133)

However, as Anderson (1996) has pointed out, the tide is changing, and "the convergence and conflict between virtual and real time demands on professional time is emerging even at the face-to-face conference" (p. 133). Mobile technologies are permeating the walls of the traditional conference centers and the distractions that are prevalent in online conferences now exist for participants of f2f conferences. These delegates are now very likely to be inundated with e-mails and phone calls from work and home while attending a conference thousands of miles away. "This reversal of roles illustrates the convergence of time management concerns and the demands on time, when we begin to work and learn in both the real and the virtual world" (Anderson, 1996, p. 133).

Conclusion

It is generally believed that online conferences will not replace physical conferences (Minshull, 2004; Sierra, 2007; Wang, 1999). However, the benefits afforded by online conferencing make it a viable alternative, one that has the potential to alleviate issues of cost, effectiveness, and accessibility. In order for this potential to be released, conference organizers need to understand the advantages and disadvantages presented by the three generations of online conferences and align the associated technologies in a complementary fashion with the objectives of the conference and the needs of the participants. In addition, online conference organizers, through the innovative use of these technologies, must provide for "dynamic, authentic, practice-based, collaborative, and future-oriented" educational opportunities (Mott, 2000). The effectiveness of online conferences is dependent upon appropriate choice of technology (Chapters 3 & 4), thoughtful pedagogical design (Chapters 5 & 6), and implementation (Chapters 8 & 9).

3

Technologies

From Text to Immersion

Introduction

With each passing year, more technologies are added to the assortment of
tools available to online conference organizers, presenters and participants.
These tools offer improvements and variety to the ways in which online conferences may be organized and attended. Each of these technological tools
has its advantages and disadvantages for online conferences, and some of
these technologies lend themselves to a particular pedagogical purpose.
Consequently, many online conferences now use a "mashup" approach that
integrates the three generations of online conferencing technologies. By
doing so, conferences can be structured in such a way as to take advantage
of the strengths offered by each of these generations while minimizing the
weaknesses. These tools provide the means by which continuing professional education (CPE) conferences may be transformed by improving accessibility and increasing interaction, both during and after the conference
proceedings. However, for this to happen, stakeholders must be aware of
the affordances of these technologies and use them accordingly.

Online Conferences: Professional Development for a Networked Era, pages 27–46
Copyright © 2010 by Information Age Publishing
27

This chapter discusses many of the technologies currently used in online CPE conferences and provides examples of their application. Many of these technologies have been employed with great success for purposes that were not originally intended, and thus their use can be described as socially constructed. The chapter is organized into four sections:

- Online Conferencing Platforms
- One-way Presentation Media
- Asynchronous Interactive Technologies, including Web 2.0
- Synchronous Interactive Technologies, including MUVEs

The first section provides a description of the various platform configurations and tools that are available to conference organizers. The following three sections look at the technologies used to present content and support interaction. Information on specific platforms and software that are frequently employed within online CPE conferences was retrieved from company Web sites and is included here with the corresponding Web links. However, it is beyond the scope of this chapter to list the multitude of technologies that lend themselves to the purpose of presenting information and interacting online. To assist in the selection of such software, we have included a list of Web sites that provide names, links, and evaluations of both commercial and open-source conferencing software at the end of the chapter.

The Conference Platform

Online conference platforms (sometimes referred to as communities) may be structured in various configurations using a wide assortment of tools. At one end of the spectrum are the hosted, proprietary platforms that offer an all-in-one conferencing package. Although the features that are included may vary, the most comprehensive platforms include the following:

- Configurable site in terms of look, feel, and functionality
  - Allows for branding and customized appearance
  - Choice of features to be included
  - Allows for embedding of multimedia files
  - Enables conference organizers to set different access rights and permissions
  - Enables some participant choice regarding settings
  - Multi-Language User Interface
- Home/Welcome page
  - Used to provide orientation and instruction to new users via text or embedded video

- May include:
  - Registration/Log-In
  - Announcements (May be pushed out to external email)
  - Conference schedule
  - Description of conference keynotes
  - Links to conference pages and related sites
  - Sponsor names and links
  - Contact and emergency help information

■ Profiles, Member Directory, and Search Features
  - Participants may choose to complete some or all of their personal profile (this is mandatory for some online conferences)
  - Profiles are made available to other conference participants in a Member Directory
  - Search feature enables users to find other participants according to profile criteria
  - Enables participants to find others with similar interests, vocations, geographic location, or other commonalities

■ Live Conference Room
  - Allows for live multimedia presentations
  - Enables live meetings (usually with voice interaction) between two or more participants
  - Audio may be mediated via a standard telephone conference call or Voice over Internet Protocol (VoIP)
  - Audience communication is enabled through text and/or audio

■ Discussion forums
  - Threaded text discussion forums provide for asynchronous interaction
  - Often, topics are established by organizers according to conference themes or keynote presentations
  - New topics may be started by both conference organizers and participants

■ Live chat rooms
  - Allows for synchronous text chat between two or more participants
  - May be scheduled or spontaneous

■ Blogs
  - Allows participants to post articles, stories, and strategies
  - Can be public or restricted to predefined groups

■ Polls and Surveys
  - May be used to take votes or to get feedback from delegates

▪ Wikis
  – Enable group collaboration in the creation of conference-related material
▪ Document/Resource Library
  – An area that promotes sharing of conference-related content
  – Enables uploading and downloading of multimedia files
▪ Evaluation/Quiz tools
  – May be used for pre and post tests
  – May be used to evaluate learning for certification
  – May be used for conference evaluation
▪ Messaging System
  – Internal email allows participants to contact one another privately
  – May be forwarded to external email
▪ Content Search
  – Enables content search into the site, including posts, attachments, and uploaded files
▪ Help desk
  – Technical support for participants

Prices for hosted conference platforms vary greatly, depending upon the size and length of the conference, the features included, and the services required. For example, prices for the online Global Conference Centre hosted by *iCohere* start at $10,000 USD. *iCohere* (www.icohere.com) provides a very robust, scaleable commercial conference platform. In addition, they offer comprehensive consultation services for the organization and delivery of eLearning events. *Web Crossing* (www.webcrossing.com), a leading producer of online collaboration platforms, provides hosting packages that range from $65 per month to $2,495 per month, depending on the features used and number of users. Their prices do not include conference consultation services beyond technical support, and the platform does not include synchronous conference rooms beyond live text chat.

On the other end of the price spectrum, there are platforms available freely as open-source software. The most commonly used open-source platform is *Moodle* (http://moodle.org/). *Moodle* is a learning management system generally used for the creation of Internet-based courses and Web sites. By changing some of the language used on the platform—for example, changing *student* to *participant*—conference organizers have re-purposed this platform for use in online CPE conferences. The *Moodle* platform provides many of the features described above, including forum discussions, blogs, and wikis. However, like *Web Crossing*, it does not include synchronous conference rooms beyond live text chat. In addition, *Moodle* itself does not provide hosting services, though there are many vendors offering to set up and customize *Moodle* sites for online conference use. *Moodle* can, however, be installed on an organizer's own Web server for very low cost. *Moodle* can be installed on any computer that runs PHP and can support an SQL-type database or can be installed on the server of a Web hosting company.

Another open-source software that has been re-purposed as an online conference platform is *WordPress* (http://wordpress.org/). *WordPress* is a blog publishing platform that has grown to be the largest self-hosted blogging tool in the world. *WordPress* is completely customizable, comes with a variety of features, and allows for plug-ins that extend the core functionality. Like *Moodle*, *Wordpress* must be installed on a webhost.

The Mashup

It is rare for an online conference to rely solely on a single platform. In most cases, online conferences are put together using a mashup of technologies and platforms. For example, many online conferences that have used *Web Crossing*, *Moodle*, or *Wordpress* for presentation of text content and asynchronous communication have supplemented these platforms with live conferencing software such as *Elluminate* (www.elluminate.com/), *iVocalize* (https://www.ivocalize.com/), or *Adobe Acrobat Connect* (www.adobe.com/products/acrobatconnect/), which are used for real time activities. In some cases, the conference platform is simply a Web site that links to content, presentations, and interactive software that is hosted elsewhere (see Figure 3.1). The Web site supports the organization of the distributed conference and serves as a portal. An example of this type of dispersed online CPE conference is ODR Cyberweek (http://www.odr.info/cyberweek2008/). ODR Cyberweek is an online conference that explores the application of technology to online dispute resolution. It has been held online since 1999.

Some online conferences have two Web sites. The first serves as a promotional site. This site may be used to announce the conference, solicit presentation submissions, and provide a description of the program and keynote speakers. This site may also be used to process conference registration and provide access to the second site, the actual conference platform (see Figure 3.2). In this example, the conference platform is more comprehensive, including some of the features listed above.

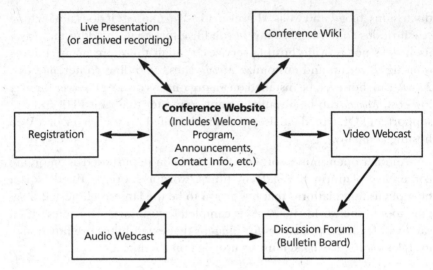

Figure 3.1 A dispersed online conference configuration.

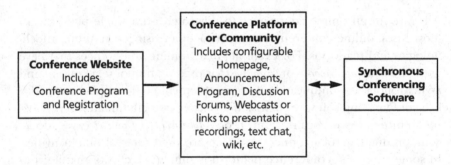

Figure 3.2 A centralized online conference configuration.

One-Way Media Used to Present Content

Interaction between and amongst the facilitators, presenters, and participants is a key component of online CPE conferences (Anderson, 1996). However, many online conferences utilize one-way media, such as text or webcasts, to present content. One-way presentations like these do not by themselves constitute an online conference event. However, they are commonly used to provide a learning opportunity and a basis for discussion. This discussion may take place synchronously or asynchronously after the content has been viewed by conference delegates.

Presentations that are webcast may use audio or video. One form of webcast frequently used in online conferences displays a PowerPoint presentation accompanied by an audio recording of the presenter. This type of presentation is often referred to as an online poster session. Recordings of synchronous presentations represent another form of webcast. Most online conferences post these recordings on the conference Web site so that participants may view the session at a time that is convenient for them. These webcasts not only provide a recording of the presentation, but allow the participant to view the recorded interactions between the audience and the presenter. As in any learning/teaching situation, the choice of media should be influenced by the goals of the presentation, the characteristics of the audience, and the accessibility of the technology.

There are many commercial software packages available that aid in the creation of webcasts. The simplest of these allow the creator to record and edit an audio presentation. More advanced software packages support the creation of multimedia presentations (see Table 3.1). Many free and open-source software options for the production of webcasts also exist, including *SlideShare, Audacity,* and *DimDim Free. SlideShare* is a presentation-sharing site that can be used to synch audio to PowerPoint slides to create a *slidecast.* The slidecast can then be embedded on a conference Web site. *DimDim Free* can be used as both a synchronous conferencing platform for up to 20 users and a presentation creation tool. It allows presenters to record their presentations on a live platform and then embed the recording on a blog or Web site. Table 3.2 provides links to these and other free presentation platforms. Open-source software options can also be found online at The Free Software Directory (http://directory.fsf.org/). This directory catalogues free software that runs under free operating systems, particularly the GNU operating system and its GNU/Linux variants.

Asynchronous Technologies

Asynchronous conferencing technologies enable interaction between and amongst the presenters and participants at a time that is convenient for the user. Although both audio (voice mail) and video (video mail) can be used, asynchronous interaction is most commonly achieved using text. The following is a list of asynchronous technologies commonly used within online CPE conferences to support communication and collaboration.

Email

The earliest asynchronous conferencing technology was email. The first online conferences used mailing lists to distribute text presentations and support subsequent discussions (Anderson, 1996). Email continues to be used in online conferences, but its role has changed. Today, email is

TABLE 3.1 Commercial Multimedia Presentation Software

Product, Price and URL	Description
Adobe Captivate 4 $799 USD http://www.adobe.com/products/captivate/	Author eLearning content with advanced interactivity, software and scenario simulations, quizzes, and other engaging experiences.
Adobe Presenter 7 $500 USD http://www.adobe.com/products/presenter/	Converts PowerPoint content to Flash, retaining animations and transitions. Add narration, animations, interactivity, quizzes, software simulations, and embed video. Scorm and AICC compliant. Adobe PDF file publication.
Articulate Presenter '09 $699 USD http://www.articulate.com/	Converts PowerPoint content to Flash, retaining animations and transitions. May be extended with customizable players, audio narrations, interactivity, and embedded video. Scorm and AICC compliant. Multiple publishing options: Web, CD, MS Word, or podcasts.
BB FlashBack Pro $199 USD http://www.bbsoftware.co.uk/BBFlashBack.aspx	Lets you record the screen, sound, and video taken from your webcam simultaneously. Share recordings online and save them as AVI and Flash movies. Adds annotation and WMV and QuickTime exporting. Adds audio and video editing, EXE export, and zoom and pan effects.
Camtasia Studio $299 USD http://www.techsmith.com/camtasia.asp	Records on-screen activity, including PowerPoint presentations. Allows editing, including adding narration and sharing. Produces video in a wide variety of formats and sizes, including HD.

TABLE 3.2 Free Presentation Software

Audio Tools

Audacity http://audacity.sourceforge.net/	Audacity® is free, open-source software for recording and editing sounds. It is available for Mac OS X, Microsoft Windows, GNU/Linux, and other operating systems.

Multimedia Presentations

BB Flashback Express http://www.bbsoftware.co.uk/BBFlashBack_FreePlayer.aspx	Record your screen, sound, and video taken from your webcamsimultaneously. Share movies with one-click upload to *YouTube* and other video sharing sites. Save movies as Flash or AVI files.
Dimdim Free http://www.dimdim.com/products/dimdim_editions_free.html	*Dimdim* is a browser-based Web conferencing service. You can show presentations, collaborate via whiteboards, chat, talk, and broadcast via webcam with absolutely no download required to host, attend, or even record meetings.
SlideShare http://www.slideshare.net/	Upload and share your PowerPoint presentations and Word documents on *SlideShare*. Share publicly or privately. Add audio to make a webinar.
VirtualDub http://www.virtualdub.org/index.html	*VirtualDub* is a video capture/processing utility for 32-bit Windows platforms (95/98/ME/NT4/2000/XP), licensed under the GNU General Public License (GPL).
Windows Movie Maker http://www.microsoft.com/windowsxp/using/moviemaker/default.mspx	*Windows Movie Maker* is a free video-editing tool included with Microsoft Windows XP and VISTA. Turn home movies into videos that can be shared across the Internet or burned to a CD or DVD.
Wink: http://debugmode.com/wink/	*Wink* is a tutorial and presentation creation software, primarily aimed at creating tutorials on how to use software (e.g., a tutorial for MS-Word or Excel). Using *Wink*, you can capture screenshots; add explanations, boxes, buttons, titles, et cetera; and generate a highly effective tutorial for your users.

rarely used to present content. It is most commonly used by conference organizers as a medium for communication before, during, and after the conference for the following purposes:

- Call for papers
- Communications with presenters
- Promoting the conference
- Announcements before and during the conference
- Contact/Help for conference participants
- Post-conference evaluation

Email also supports interaction within conference discussion forums. Many online conferencing platforms enable email push out of announcements and forum postings. Participants may subscribe to a conference forum and receive email updates whenever a new posting to the forum is made. In some cases, responses may also be posted via email. Finally, most online conferences encourage continued interaction and networking between participants after the conference ends. This is done by providing participants with a space where they can post their contact information, including email addresses.

Text Messaging (SMS)

In many parts of the world, text messaging or SMS has become a pervasive part of communication culture. Conference organizers, such as Direct Learn, have begun to take advantage of this trend by using SMS to communicate with conference participants (Judith Mole, personal communication, Sept. 17, 2008). As SMS is limited to 160 characters, these communications are usually brief reminders of upcoming conference events. Text messaging for this purpose is generally one-way, but serves to encourage participation and interaction in the conference.

Bulletin Boards/Forums

Threaded bulletin boards provide a public area for discussion of conference presentations and/or common areas of interest. Although audio is possible, most conference bulletin boards use text as the medium of choice. Text discussion boards provide maximum accessibility, as they do not require a high bandwidth. Threaded discussions enable participants to engage in a topic already under discussion or to start a new one. New topics appear in a separate thread so that they are not lost in a mass of postings. Unlike email, a participant may respond to any item in the thread and his or her response or question will be displayed and archived in relation to the comment (usually immediately following) the post that triggered his or her response. Many bulletin boards also support interaction and sharing by allowing participants to add attachments, insert links, and embed multimedia files.

Bulletin boards are a common component of most conferencing platforms, but they are also available as stand-alone software. Although there are many free and open-source bulletin boards available, commercial providers continue to exist. These providers offer the added benefit of hosting services, technical support, and an abundance of features. Features that are common to most conferencing forums include: polls, attachments, private messaging, event calendars, paid subscriptions, customizable templates, IP and email banning, bad word filters, emoticons/smilies, multiple languages, search capability, differentiated user groups, flexible permissions system, multiple moderators, board traffic stats, and email and forum support services.

Asynchronous conferencing platforms do differ in the degree of control, automation, and customization afforded. Not-so-common features include: auto install and upgrade, WSIWYG editor, integrated spell checker, RSS export and import of content, and the ability to read forums via email (Anderson & McCarthy, 2005).

Prices for commercial bulletin boards vary widely. Leased licenses start at $5 per month for a standard conferencing forum that is hosted on a local server, while purchased licenses start as low as $99. If a local server is not available or compatible with the conferencing platform, most commercial providers will host the forum remotely on their own server for an additional cost. The cost of hosting may vary according to the amount of disk space required. In addition, prices vary depending upon the technical support that is required. Many companies charge extra for more rapid (phone) technical support and tech support beyond the initial setup period. Finally, organizations choosing to purchase a license, as opposed to leasing, may have to pay for future upgrades of the conferencing platform.

Web 2.0 Technologies

In recent years, Web 2.0 technologies, many of which are available for free on the Internet, have been used for various purposes within online conferences.

> Web 2.0 refers to a perceived second generation of web development and design that facilitates communication, secure information sharing, interoperability, and collaboration on the World Wide Web. Web 2.0 concepts have led to the development and evolution of web-based communities, hosted services, and applications. Examples include social-networking sites, video-sharing sites, wikis, blogs, and tags. (Web 2.0, 2009)

Conference organizers have found innovative uses for these technologies. In this section, we will briefly describe some of the Web 2.0 technologies listed above and look at how these technologies have been used in online conferences to date.

Wikis

A wiki is a collection of Web pages that allows anyone with access to contribute or modify content. Wikis have been used in online conferences for collaboration and sharing between participants. For example, at the Shaping our Future (SOF) Online Conference, 2008, (http://scope.bccampus. ca/course/view.php?id=56) delegates contributed to a wiki that overviewed components, methodologies, important research questions, and next steps towards creating a pan-Canadian research agenda.

Social Networking Sites

Social networking sites focus on "building online communities of people who share interests and/or activities, or who are interested in exploring the interests and activities of others" (Social Networking, 2009). For the most part, these social networking sites have been used to promote online conferences by spreading the word. However, recently these sites have seen more integral usage in online conferences. For example, *Ning* (http:// www.ning.com/) has been used as both a conference platform (Connecting Online C009 Conference: http://connecting-online.ning.com/) and as a presentation and discussion area linked to from a separate conference platform (K–12 Online Conference: http://k12onlineconference.org/).

Tags

Many Web 2.0 applications, such as social networking sites, blogs, and video/slide sharing sites, enable conference organizers, presenters, and participants to post and share conference-related content outside of the conference parameters. Consequently, most online conference organizers now create or suggest a tag that is used to identify conference-related content on the Web. A conference tag should be short (to facilitate use) but must also be unique, such that non-conference-related material is not included in conference searches. A common tag would be the initials of the conference followed by the year (for example, *SOF2008*, used for the Shaping our Future online conference held in 2008). Searching for the tag then allows users or conference organizers to retrieve and aggregate on the conference site all the postings related to the conference.

Search services such as *Technorati* or *Google* can be used to find and aggregate this content on one page. Some conference Web sites now include feeds to tagged content. The SOF2008 conference Web site linked to a *Pageflake*, where tagged content from various sources was aggregated for the participants. *Pageflakes* is a customizable homepage that allows the user to set up feeds from favorite sites and blogs. The SOF2008 *Pageflake* provided feeds on tagged conference material from *SlideShare, Twitter,* and *del.icio.us.* It also included a widget that searched blogs for the SOF2008 tag. "Regardless of conference format, the use of a conference tag enables attendees to locate conference-related content and each other" (Siemens, Tittenberger, & Anderson, 2008).

Blogs

Many online conference participants choose to comment about presentations and content on their own blogs rather than within the provided forums. This leads to discussions outside of the formal conference platform. As mentioned above, conference organizers should recommend a tag that may be used to retrieve these dispersed blog posts.

Twitter (http://twitter.com/), a micro-blogging service, has also been used by conference presenters and participants for conference promotion and serves as a type of "back-channel" interaction. Conference organizers may create or suggest a *Twitter* hashtag (in *Twitter,* any word that begins with the "#" character is a searchable tag). Then participants can subscribe to (or follow) the conference tag. Anyone may then post a comment of up to 140 characters to that account, and it will be relayed to all account subscribers.

Video and Slide Sharing Sites

Video and slide sharing sites such as *YouTube* (www.youtube.com/) and *Slideshare* (www.slideshare.net/) may be used by online conference presenters to store and stream webcasts or the slides of presentations. Participants may also use these sites to find other related material. Video and slide sharing sites provide another reason for creating a conference tag that participants and organizers can use to identify conference-related activities, commentaries, and artifacts.

Synchronous Technologies

Synchronous conferencing technologies support real-time interaction via text, audio, or video. Also included under this umbrella are third-generation conferencing technologies. These immersive 3D environments not only provide real-time communication via text or audio, they also allow participants to express themselves through their avatars' gestures and facial expressions. The following is a brief description of some of the synchronous conferencing technologies used in online CPE conferences.

Live Text Chat (Instant Messaging)

Live text chatting has become a prevalent form of communication amongst young people. It is also used extensively in online CPE conferences for a variety of purposes. Live text chats with conference presenters may be scheduled after participants have had an opportunity to read or view content that has been presented using one-way media. Text chats may also be used in conjunction with a live multimedia presentation. This provides a means of communication for those participants without microphones and allows for chat amongst participants during the live presentation. Finally, many conferences provide live chat rooms for participants to use as a social meeting place. These rooms promote the type of communication and networking that might occur in the hallway after a traditional presentation or in the bar later in the day. Meetings and social gatherings in these live chat rooms may occur spontaneously, be initiated by participants, or be scheduled by the conference organizers.

Live chat rooms are often included in both commercial and open-source conferencing platforms. However, a live chat room may also be attained as stand-alone software, and most IM tools are now available free of charge.

Live Web Conferencing

Use of live Web conferencing platforms for CPE presentations has grown in response to increased accessibility to greater bandwidth and increasing functionality of Web conferencing platforms. These platforms allow for a live audio presentation to learners logged into a central Web site. Audio may be distributed via a standard telephone conference call or by VoIP. The simplest of these platforms uses screen sharing in conjunction with teleconferencing. More advanced platforms allow for multiple presenters in different locations and provide some or all of the following features:

- Live video via webcams
- Shared, interactive whiteboards
- Downloading and sharing of PowerPoint presentations and images
- Application sharing
- Interactive quiz or polling features
- Instant messaging
- Breakout rooms
- File transfer

- Multimedia playback of video and audio
- Web tours
- Multi-language translations

Costs for these live conferencing rooms vary according to the features included, the hosting requirements, and the size of the conference. At present, open-source and free software options offer few of the features listed above and are limited to a small number of concurrent users. Unfortunately, most commercial providers of Web conferencing software do not list prices on their Web sites. Contracts are usually negotiated on an individual basis. However, many commercial providers offer free Web conferencing rooms for limited numbers of users, and most offer special rates to educational institutions and organizations. In addition, some commercial providers have, in the past, entered into sponsorship agreements with online conference organizers and provided their platform free of charge for a limited time.

Participation in a Web conference usually requires each user to install a program or plug-in to their Web browser. This may involve the installation of a standalone program, often delivered automatically as a java program or with less trouble as a browser plug-in (typically Flash). These installations may cause participants problems if their machines are protected from external programs (these programs can be used to infect machines with viruses) or if the Web conferencing program requires use of dedicated ports that may be restricted in schools or commercial offices. Thus, it is important for organizers to use tools that are as easily installed as possible and that are supported by help desks and testing sites by the conference platform vendor. It is also important for organizers to offer test or warm-up events prior to opening conference activities in which participants can test and configure as necessary their local machines.

Video

Video may be used in several ways to support interaction in online conferences. For example, conference presenters and participants may use webcams to stream video of themselves, providing facial familiarity. Recorded video clips may be streamed onto a Web conferencing platform to enhance a live presentation. Finally, live or recorded video of a face-to-face presentation may be streamed to an audience in a synchronous Web conferencing platform. Many dual-mode conferences (supporting both face-to-face and online participants) are enabled in this way. For example, the 2008 American Society of Association Executives (ASAE) Conference held in Washington, DC, was videotaped and streamed to online participants. Interaction between the participants in Washington and the online participants was facilitated by moderators on site using two-way conference calling, while interaction between the online participants was supported over the Web via text and VoIP (Association Trends, 2008). To date, video conferencing has been used sparingly in online CPE conferences, as access is limited by the expense of enlisting the technical crew on site and the need for broadband Internet connection by all participants.

Multi-User Virtual Environments: Second Life

Many of the conference centers that have been built in *Second Life* have been modeled after traditional face-to-face venues, with a stage, screen, and participant seating (see Figure 3.3). Likewise, presentations often mimic those experienced in real life. Avatars, standing on a stage, deliver a PowerPoint or video presentation. Communication between the presenter and participants is encouraged after the presentation and supported by VoIP and/or text chat. In 1996, Anderson noted that "Early applications of virtual conferences imitated, or were modeled upon the face-to-face conference" (p. 122). This "horseless carriage" approach has been repeated with each new generation of online conference. However, as understanding and experience with each generation has grown, conference organizers, presenters, and participants have experimented with new ways to coordinate,

Figure 3.3 NMC's Symposium on New Media & Learning; March 24–26, 2009 at the NMC Campus in Second Life.

present, and partake in online conferences. This is also, gradually, becoming true of *Second Life.*

Second Life has been used as a platform to enable dual-mode conferences. For these conferences, audio and/or video is streamed from a live presentation into *Second Life*, where participants engage in the presentation online. A PowerPoint presentation may also be loaded into *Second Life* so that online participants can see everything that their live counterparts are seeing (see Figure 3.4). A facilitator who is present in both the live presentation and *Second Life* supports interaction between the two by relaying questions from the *Second Life* audience. Online conference organizers have also used *Second Life* as an area for social gatherings. For example, the 2008 TCC Worldwide Online Conference (http://tcc.kcc. hawaii.edu/2009/tcc/welcome.html) held a reception at the end of each day on the NMC Campus in *Second Life.* To date, few conferences have been held entirely in *Second Life.* However, as its popularity grows, this is likely to change.

Figure 3.4   NMC's Impact of Digital Media Symposium; October 21, 2006, at the NMC Campus in Second Life.

Looking to the Future

Online communication technologies are evolving rapidly, making it difficult to write about current technological use without sounding behind the times. While doing this research, the authors came across many blogs and articles describing new technologies that held great potential for future use in online CPE conferences. We would like to close this chapter with a brief discussion of just a few of these.

Many of the new innovations are actually mashups of currently existing technologies, offering the benefits of different types of communication within one platform. For example, Google announced the soon-to-be-released *Google Wave*, "a new model for communication and collaboration on the web" (Google, 2009). This platform is "a hybrid of email, web chat, IM, and project management software" (Parr, 2009). *Google Wave*'s features include:

- Real-time communication: In most instances, you can see what someone else is typing, character-by-character.
- Embeddability: *Waves* can be embedded on any blog or Web site.
- Applications and extensions: Just like a *Facebook* application or an *iGoogle* gadget, developers can build their own apps within waves. They can be anything from bots to complex real-time games.
- Wiki functionality: *Anything* written within a *Google Wave* can be edited by anyone else because all conversations within the platform are shared. Thus, you can correct information, append information, or add your own commentary within a developing conversation.
- Open-source: The *Google Wave* code will be open-source in order to foster innovation and adoption amongst developers.
- Playback: You can playback any part of the wave to see what was said.
- Natural language: *Google Wave* can autocorrect your spelling, even going as far as knowing the difference between similar words, like "been" and "bean." It can also auto-translate on-the-fly.
- Drag-and-drop file sharing: No attachments; just drag your file and drop it inside *Google Wave* and everyone will have access (Parr, 2009).

Other mashups offering great potential for online conferencing integrate virtual worlds with learning management systems. The most advanced of these mashups is *Sloodle* (http://www.sloodle.org/moodle/). *Sloodle* is an open-source project that provides a *Moodle* module, which communicates with interactive 3D *Sloodle* teaching tools inside *Second Life*. *Sloodle* provides a complete package of tools that allow users to work with *Moodle* activities in *Second Life*. *Sloodle* also offers tools that help users to register on the site and check user permissions. In addition, *Sloodle* developers are working on making *Sloodle* compatible with virtual worlds based on the *OpenSimulator* (http://opensimulator.org) platform. *OpenSimulator* (OpenSim) is an open-source server platform that allows anyone to host their own *Second Life*-like virtual world (Sulčič, 2009).

Finally, an increasing number of virtual worlds are being developed such that they can be accessed within a regular browser, thus enabling conference organizers, presenters, or even participants to create a virtual space and add links to it within the conference Web site. Conference organizers may also choose to embed the virtual world within the site (Sulčič, 2009). Users may then enter and enjoy the benefits of the 3D space without the need for additional plug-ins. Several of these virtual worlds also allow users to link to other Web sites and add media such as *YouTube* videos, mp3 files and *Flickr* pictures. Examples of browser-based virtual worlds include:

- Vivaty: http://www.vivaty.com/
- Club Cooee: http://www.clubcooee.com/
- ExitReality: http://www.exitreality.com/about.html
- MetaPlace: https://www.metaplace.com/

TABLE 3.3 Listings and Evaluations of Presentation Software and Online Conferencing Software

Centre for Learning and Performance Technologies	http://www.c4lpt.co.uk/Directory/Tools/im.html
Capterra	http://www.capterra.com/web-collaboration-software
e-Learning Centre	http://www.e-learningcentre.co.uk/eclipse/vendors/index.html#ab
The Free Software Directory	http://directory.fsf.org/
Thinkofit.com	http://www.thinkofit.com/webconf/index.htm

Conclusion

This chapter is intended to raise awareness and understanding of the range of technologies available for the design and delivery of online CPE conferences. Examples of how these technologies have been used were provided so that readers might benefit from the experiences of others and be inspired by the innovative applications of technologies not originally intended for use in online conferences. However, decisions regarding the choice of technology to use should always be dictated by the goals of the conference/presentation, the characteristics and capacities of the participants, and the affordances of the technology. The next chapter examines these affordances more closely by reviewing the advantages and disadvantages of both synchronous and asynchronous conferencing technologies.

4

Synchronous versus Asynchronous Conferencing Technologies

Introduction

Although advances in technology have provided the opportunity for synchronous conferences with excellent audio and visual capabilities that closely parallel face-to-face (f2f), many online conference organizers continue to utilize asynchronous text conferencing tools alone or in conjunction with synchronous media. This is due to the unique and often complimentary affordances of both types of computer mediated communication (CMC). Unfortunately, studies documenting these advantages and disadvantages in the context of continuing professional education (CPE) conferences are extremely limited. Most of the literature pertaining to synchronous and asynchronous CMC is based on the experiences of learners within higher academic courses. However, many of the benefits and limitations documented in this literature may be generalized to other contexts. For this reason, this literature is included in this section in the hopes that it may shed light on the affordances of these technologies to online conferences for CPE.

Online Conferences: Professional Development for a Networked Era, pages 47–53
Copyright © 2010 by Information Age Publishing
All rights of reproduction in any form reserved.

47

Synchronous Conferencing

Advantages

Synchronous conferences have been credited with providing "a sense of immediacy and spontaneity" (Anderson, 1996, p. 126) as well as a higher level of social presence compared to asynchronous conferencing (Pena-Shaff, Martin, & Gay, 2001). Audio communication within synchronous platforms further enhances the feeling of social presence by adding verbal cues to the interaction. In an article describing the experiences of students in a graduate studies course utilizing both synchronous and asynchronous text communications, Schwier & Balbar (2002), found that synchronous communication "promoted a strong sense of community" amongst the learners. The synchronous sessions were "characterized by dynamic exchanges, and there was often passion about an issue expressed that generated an equally passionate response." They credited these interactions with energizing the students and instructors.

Immersive worlds, such as *Second Life*, further enrich the advantages of synchronous communication by providing participants with a sense of self and a sense of space that imitates real life (Cross, O'Driscoll, & Trondsen, 2007). Studies have shown that humans respond to avatars in virtual environments in ways similar to the physical world in terms of personal space and social presence (Bailenson, Blascovich, Beall, & Loomis, 2003). Virtual worlds have also been credited with fostering a culture of collaborative learning (Bronack et al., 2008). Finally, virtual worlds offer educators environments and experiences not possible in the real world. Continuing education events can, potentially, take place in *Second Life* operating rooms, airports, or courtrooms that provide visualizations of structures and events that are multidimensional. These life-like simulations create a sense of authenticity and engagement that is rarely found in classroom- or text-based forms of CPE. The locations and experiences available in immersive environments are limited only by the developer's imagination and technical capabilities.

Disadvantages

The greatest drawback of synchronicity is the obvious requirement of "dispersed participants (often straddling many time zones) to participate at the same time" (Anderson, 1996, 126). Recently, virtual conference organizers have come up with unique ways to deal with the issue of disparate time zones. The 2007 NMC Symposium on Creativity in *Second Life* (http://www.nmc.org/symposium-on-creativity) addressed this issue through the use of live, interactive breakout sessions scheduled at times that were convenient to participants from differing time zones. In 2007 and 2008, the Megaconference (http://www.megaconference.org/) ran for 13 hours straight. Presenters from various countries hosted online sessions at times that were suitable to their respective time zones.

Several other limitations of synchronous conferencing have been identified. The first of these limitations is the issue of increased cognitive load (Van Bruggen, Kirschner, & Jochems, 2002). In a discussion of Net-based collaborative learning, Hron and Friedrich (2003) point out that synchronous CMC, "makes great demands on its learners, who must operate a complex technology, deal with an often complex subject matter, as well as communicate with other learners at the same time" (p. 72). This issue is especially prevalent in synchronous text conferences where the ability to respond quickly is critical to participation in the conference and coherence in the discussion. This challenge is exacerbated in that more than one topic can be discussed at the same time with little support from the technology for separating different conversations from each other. Schwier and Balbar (2002) noted that "students felt isolated by the difficulty of trying to do so many different types of things simultaneously: processing the ideas presented by others, thinking about a response, composing a response, and typing a response." They point out that threads of conversation can be difficult to follow, "especially when there [are] several dyadic conversations occurring at the same time." This confusion can be confounded by the lack of nonverbal cues and the difficulty in interpreting the intentions of others (Day, 1996; Hron & Friedrich, 2003; Schwier & Balbar, 2002). In addition, Schwier and Balbar (2002) state that participation in synchronous text conferences is influenced by the technical and typing skills of the learners.

It is also quite common for different forms of synchronous, and even asynchronous, technologies to be used concurrently. Our experience moderating Web conferences, which have extensive text and twitter backchannel activity, has proven to be an exhausting activity and often leaves participants with a feeling (which is often accurate) that they have missed something. Although much attention has been given to the so-called multitasking (or more likely, multiple partial attention) capabilities of the "Net generation," there is increasing evidence of the cost and cognitive overload associated with multiple synchronous streams. Although use of *Twitter*, instant messaging, and other external tools is beyond the control of conference organizers, care should be taken not to overwhelm and distract conference participants by too much simultaneous synchronous activity that is generated by the conference organizers.

Finally, both Kasser (2001) and Schwier and Balbar (2002) identified the technical weakness of synchronous conferences, that being the necessity for the communication links to work properly at all sites at the same time. In an asynchronous conference, a temporary delay due to technical difficulties at any point in the interaction amongst presenter and participants has little effect on the conference as a whole. Whereas a similar delay in a synchronous conference may mean the end of the particular event or, at the very least, may cause participants to miss scheduled events.

Asynchronous Conferencing

Asynchronous text conferencing in the context of academic courses has grown in popularity over the last decade in both distance education programs and blended programs. Consequently, this mode of CMC has received more attention from researchers than has synchronous communication. The literature concerning asynchronous conferencing in this context is rich in descriptions of the advantages and disadvantages afforded by this mode of online communication. Asynchronous text-based conferences are characterized by two unique features: temporal flexibility and the lack of social presence. However, these features present a double-edged sword.

Temporal Flexibility

The most commonly cited advantage of asynchronous conferencing is the temporal convenience that it affords. Asynchronous conferencing technologies allow participants flexibility and control over the time they spend in the conference. As Anderson (1996) points out, "delegates have the freedom to shift the time devoted to the conference to mesh with individual time availability" (p. 132). More to the point, Wang (1999), states, "They can leave a presentation at any time or for any reasons; run an errand, visit the bathroom and get a beverage. They can always come back to catch up from where they left" (p. 70). In addition, participants are not forced to choose between two or more conference presentations that are running simultaneously (Kasser, 2001; Minshull, 2006; Wang, 1999). Unfortunately, the temporal convenience afforded by asynchronous conferences also poses challenges for participants in the form of delays in message exchange (Burge, 1994; Hew & Cheung, 2003). This latency in message exchange, according to Hron and Friedrich (2003), affects the contextual structure and coherence of the discussions, as "multiple and interwoven lines of argumentation can result" (p. 72).

Another commonly cited advantage provided by temporal flexibility is the increased opportunity for interaction, as all participants may contribute without the constraints of time or the rules of social interaction (Dennis, 2004; Schwan, Straub, & Hesse, 2002). Asynchronous online discussion forums are generally available 24 hours a day for the duration of the conference. During that time, participants may post comments or questions as they see fit. Unlike f2f and moderated audio conferences, there is no smooth turn-taking of speakers and more than one topic may be addressed at a time (Hron & Friedrich, 2003; Murphy, 2001). "Individuals respond, not according to a pre-imposed order, but on the basis of their interest in the topic" (Murphy & Coleman, 2004). This freedom to participate when and how they choose has been credited with creating an "equalizing effect" that benefits slow and shy participants (Ortega, 1997). In a recent study of perception of asynchronous conferencing by various psychological types, Lin, Cranton, and Bridglall (2005) observed that:

> People who are more introverted and those who prefer using the thinking function fall naturally into the demands of asynchronous discussion forums. They have time to think and do not have people "in their face" waiting for a response. Meanwhile, people who see themselves as more active than reflective also find it beneficial to have time to formulate thoughts and present them in a more organized fashion than they could do on the spot in a face-to-face discussion. (p. 1810)

However, this capacity for asynchronous conferences to increase the amount of interaction can lead to "frustrating and difficult experiences for learners" (Murphy & Coleman, 2004). One of the common complaints of asynchronous forums is the vast number of postings that can accumulate and overwhelm participants (Burge, 1994; Hron & Friedrich, 2003; Wiesenberg & Hutton, 1996). In the study conducted by Murphy and Coleman (2004), some learners complained that the freedom from the rules of social interaction afforded by asynchronous conferences enabled domination of discussions by individuals and overly assertive behavior. In addition, some participants described feeling excluded, inadequate, and frustrated when their postings were unanswered or responded to in a negative manner. These comments "suggest that a lack of turn-taking or permission may not be beneficial in all contexts or under all circumstances" (Murphy & Coleman, 2004). Finally, Herring (1999) argues that these characteristics of asynchronous conferences run the risk of generating discussions that are incoherent. However, Herring (1999) points out that despite this problem, the popularity of these conferences continues to grow. She proposes two explanations for this paradox: "the ability of users to adapt to the medium, and the advantages of loosened coherence for heightened interactivity and language play" (Herring, 1999).

Finally, it has been argued that asynchronous conferences differ from synchronous not only in the quantity of interaction afforded, but also the quality of that interaction. The temporal flexibility of asynchronous conferences allows participants to contribute at their own pace. Thus, they have time to reflect on the postings and give careful consideration to the responses that they make (Berge 1999, Burge, 1994; Heckman & Annabi, 2003; Rossman, 1999; Williams, 2002). This characteristic of asynchronous conferences has been credited with producing more meaningful interaction than is possible in a f2f conference (Lapadat, 2002; Lin, Cranton, & Bridglall, 2005; Pena-Shaff et al., 2001). However, Murphy and Coleman (2004) observed that "while the medium may support more reflection, knowledge construction, and critical thinking, etc., it does not guarantee that these benefits will be achieved."

Lack of Physical Presence

Although the lack of physical presence is characteristic of all virtual conferences, synchronous or asynchronous, the degree of separation and lack of social presence is greatest in text-based asynchronous conferences. In these conferences, there are neither visual nor auditory cues to aid the participants in their communication with each other. In addition, the discourse lacks the immediacy and spontaneity evident in synchronous text-based conferences. On a positive note, it has been suggested that the absence of physical presence may reduce the influence of prejudice associated with race, gender, age, appearance, or accent (Harasim, Hiltz, Teles, & Turoff, 1995; Warschauer, 1997). However, the difficulties of communication in the absence of visual or auditory cues have been described repeatedly in the literature (Burge, 1994; Salmon, 2000; Wiesenberg & Hutton, 1996). In the study conducted by Murphy and Coleman (2004), the learners characterized the text-based asynchronous medium as one that is "impersonal, lacking in emotion, sterile, and fraught with interpretation errors." Finally, Anderson and Kanuka (1997), in a study of participant perceptions in an early asynchronous conference, found that "most participants felt that it was more difficult to socialize with other participants than in a face-to-face forum." Whether this was due to the negative effects of the temporal flexibility or the lack of physical presence, or both, is unclear. However, this data led them to ask several questions that remain pertinent today. These include:

- Can these challenges be overcome through more creative moderating techniques that foster greater collaborative learning activities or building learning communities?
- Will this be overcome as participants of online forums become more experienced with the medium?

- Are online forums creating a new kind of social form where participants will need to develop new social skills to cope with socializing electronically? If this is so, are comparisons with f2f forums really relevant or even applicable?
- Will newer technologies that support higher levels of social presence than text-based conferencing (e.g., asynchronous voice and video posting) help overcome these impediments to communication?
- Do these new forms of interacting lead to new ways of experiencing and developing learning that are not the same as f2f communities but are capable of supporting meaningful learning and satisfying social interactions?
- Or are these issues that are simply a characteristic of the medium that cannot be overcome? (Anderson & Kanuka, 1997)

Conclusion

Synchronous and asynchronous technologies each offer both advantages and disadvantages to online conference organizers and participants. An understanding of these advantages and disadvantages is beneficial to organizers deciding on which technologies to employ and how. It has been argued that while synchronous communication promotes a strong sense of community, asynchronous communication allows participants to delve into content and issues more deeply (Schwier & Balbar, 2002). Consequently, many online CPE conferences now employ a combination of the two, balancing the affordances of both.

5

Conference Components, Formats, and Design

Introduction

Online professional conferences offer numerous advantages over face-to-face (f2f) conferences. Most notably, online conferences improve accessibility to professional development events and offer greater opportunity for shared learning between dispersed professionals. However, the provision of a conference on the Web does not automatically ensure that the benefits afforded by the technologies will be realized. In order to exploit the advantages (and mitigate the disadvantages), organizers of online CPE conferences must give careful consideration to the design of the event.

Early applications of online conferences imitated the traditional model of the professional conference (Anderson, 1996). This "horseless carriage" approach has recurred with the adoption of each new generation of online conference. In fact, initial conferences in *Second Life*, the third generation of online conferences, brought the online conference nearly full circle. The virtual venues were closely modeled after traditional venues and the organizational format was usually comprised of successive speakers providing PowerPoint presentations from a stage or podium. The experience was essentially the same as one would encounter in an f2f conference, although the speakers may have possessed wings or blue hair!

As knowledge and experience in the online environment has grown, online conference organizers have begun to deviate from traditional organizational models of conferences and expand the repertoire of formats used to present information and encourage interactivity. They are learning to optimize the strengths and attributes of each generation of technology, using them in combination to produce organizational models that, in turn, realize the advantages of online conferences. Generally, these organizational models demonstrate a shift of control from the presenter to the learner.

In this chapter, we hope to assist conference organizers in the development of effective online conferences by examining the components that may be included in an online conference, describing organizational models that are currently in use, and exploring emerging trends. Finally, we discuss the design considerations that conference organizers should take into account when developing an online conference.

Components of Typical Online CPE Conferences

Many of the administrative functions of traditional conferences were the first components to be moved online and have stayed there for the sake of convenience. These components differ little whether the conference is held f2f or online. Promotion, registration, and evaluation, for example, are often completed in the same manner, using similar technologies for both traditional and online conferences. Promotion of both types of conferences usually takes place online through the use of Web site or paper advertisements, conference listings, and electronic mailing lists (email). As online promotion gains both functionality and use, more sophisticated services are becoming available to launch and support promotional campaigns. For example, *mailchimp.com* helps promoters design compelling and personalized email formats, manage lists, monitor responses, and provide other analytics gauging the success of the email promotional campaign. Registration for most conferences is supported by secure online financial services such as *PayPal* and *WorldPay*, while evaluations of conferences are usually completed using online survey tools such as *SurveyMonkey*.

Almost any aspect of a traditional f2f conference can be moved to an online venue. We have seen all of the following elements of traditional conferences offered online:

- Pre-conference workshops
- Social events
- Keynote addresses
- Presentations/concurrent sessions
- Panel discussions
- Roundtable discussions
- Breakout sessions
- Workshops
- Poster sessions
- Exhibition halls

The technologies used to provide these conference elements vary depending on the availability of the technology, the needs of the participants, and the objectives of the event. For example, keynote addresses, presentations, and poster sessions may be communicated using recorded webcasts, real-time conferencing software, or simply text documents. Workshops, roundtable discussions, and breakout sessions can be supported by Web 2.0 technologies and interactive conferencing software, while social gatherings are ideally suited to synchronous platforms and immersive worlds. However, the elements that may be included in an online conference are not limited to those listed above.

A key advantage of online conferences is not that they can provide a virtual replication of traditional conferences, but that they offer the potential for increased interaction between professionals. Consequently, most online conferences include elements that capitalize on this advantage. For instance, many online conferences include:

- Participant profiles and contact information
- Introduction forums and other online ice-breakers
- Discussion forums (lasting the duration of the conference or beyond)
- Web 2.0 applications (e.g., conference tags, RSS, wikis, etc.)
- Audience feedback, polling, and back channels during live presentations
- Picture and recorded event galleries
- Shared content archives

An added benefit to online conferences is that these elements are usually archived on the conference Web site and available to participants long after the conference has ended.

Organizational Models

As the number of platforms and tools available to online conference organizers has increased, so too has the variety of organizational models used in online conferences. Stevens and Dudeney (2009) list several popular online conferences that utilize unique approaches to providing professional development; "None is simply a repeat of another." Despite the variation that may exist, organizational models for online conferences can be differentiated along two characteristics: the interaction supported by the conference and the flexibility afforded to participants. Both of these characteristics can be represented as continuums that reflect the shift of control from conference organizers and presenters to the conference participants (see Figure 5.1).

The level of interaction and flexibility that an organizational model affords can be determined by the scheduling of conference events and the inclusion/exclusion of various conference components, technologies, and trained moderators. Figure 5.2 provides a comparison of organizational models with a focus on the level of interaction that is supported.

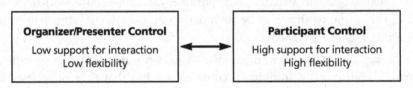

| **Organizer/Presenter Control** | | **Participant Control** |
| Low support for interaction
Low flexibility | ◀▬▶ | High support for interaction
High flexibility |

Figure 5.1 Continuum of control in online conferences.

Low Support of Interaction	**High Support of Interaction**
Little time given for interaction in synchronous events.	Ample time provided for interaction in synchronous events.
No social interaction.	Synchronous and asynchronous social gatherings are supported.
Limited opportunities for asynchronous interaction.	Unlimited opportunities of asynchronous discussion.
No discussion moderators.	Trained discussion moderators.
No Web 2.0 applications, such as tags, wikis, blogs, or social software.	Includes Web 2.0 applications and aggregators.
	Breakout rooms for more intense discussion involving special interests or smaller numbers.

Figure 5.2 Level of interaction.

In this comparison, the support given to interaction is evident in the time permitted for synchronous interaction and the opportunities provided for asynchronous interaction. The comparison also looks at the quality of that interaction by assuming that the inclusion of trained moderators will provide for better discussion. This assumption is based on our experiences in both synchronous and asynchronous discussions as well as on feedback from experienced conference organizers. Finally, the inclusion of Web 2.0 applications encourages interaction both within and outside of the conference platform. Tools such as RSS and *Twitter* enable participants to stay informed about conference activities and respond in a timely matter. Blogs and wikis, when included in the conference parameters, provide new ways for participants to interact and collaborate. And lastly, conference tags and aggregators enable participants to find and take part in conference-related conversations that are occurring outside of the conference parameters.

Figure 5.3 provides a comparison of extremes in the level of flexibility that may be afforded to participants within an online conference. In this comparison, the flexibility afforded to participants is influenced by the availability of asynchronous presentations and interaction, the scheduling of live presentations, and the variety of communication mediums provided to participants. Once again, the inclusion of Web 2.0 applications affects the level of flexibility and control afforded to participants. By including Web 2.0 applications, conference organizers provide participants with more options as to how, when, and where they will participate in the conference. However, the more one uses flexible tools, the greater the required network and hardware competencies required of both presenters and participants.

Low Flexibility	High Flexibility
Limited to synchronous presentations. No asynchronous presentations or asynchronous interaction supported.	Supports both synchronous and asynchronous presentations and interaction.
Real-time presentations scheduled during a limited block of time.	Real-time presentations offered around the clock.
Multiple real-time presentations scheduled simultaneously.	Single-track scheduling of real-time presentations.
Limited to one mode of communication.	Participants may choose their preferred communication medium.
No Web 2.0 applications, such as tags, wikis, blogs, or social software.	Includes Web 2.0 applications and aggregators.

Figure 5.3   Level of flexibility.

The following case study provides a concrete example of an organizational model that leans toward participant control. Indications of interaction and flexibility supported by the conference are analyzed based on the characteristics provided in Figures 5.2 and 5.3. Other examples of organizational models that offer different levels of interactivity and flexibility are provided throughout this text. The information on these conferences was obtained directly from the conference Web sites.

Case Study

K12 Online Conference: http://k12onlineconference.org/

The K12 Online Conference is a free online conference organized and run by volunteers and open to everyone. Conference organizers encourage participation from educators around the world interested in innovative ways Web 2.0 tools and technologies can be used to improve learning. The conference organization has evolved since its inception in 2006, and in 2009 the organizers utilized three primary sites for the conference:

- *Ning*: The organizers used this social networking site as the conversation hub. The home page included a welcome message, announcements of upcoming conference events, and a *Frappr* map (that identified the location of participants). In addition, there were dozens of links to conference related content. The *Ning* site itself not only supported the forums and groups that evolved from the conference, it also allowed participants to connect with each other through profile and contact information provided on the site. Finally, the *Ning* site served as a repository for the recorded presentations.
- **A conference blog**: This site was used to share announcements and news. The recorded presentations were also posted to this site. Participants could comment, but were not able to create new posts. The blog home page also included a welcome message and links to archived recordings from past K12 Online Conferences.
- **A conference wiki**: This site included the conference schedule and provided information to help participants and presenters get the most out of the conference. Unlike most conference wikis, it did not support collaboration. Only organizers were permitted to add content.

All conference presentations are prerecorded webcasts, 20 minutes in length or less. Only keynote presentations may exceed that time restriction. Presentations are cross-posted to both the conference blog and conference networking site (*Ning*) with supporting links and "Essential Questions." These questions are meant to encourage reflection and conversation around the presentations. Questions and comments on a presentation may be posted on the individual conference presentation blog posts, in the conference *Ning* on submitted videos, or in the *Ning* discussion forum. In addition, participants are encouraged to post about, cross-link to, and embed conference presentations and content outside of the conference parameters (using their own blogs, *Twitter*, etc.). The organizers have provided official tags to be used by participants posting conference-related content outside of the three primary conference sites.

In 2009, the theme of the conference was "Bridging the Divide." The conference was held over a two-week period in December and featured four "conference strands," two each week. The conference strands were:

- ▪ Week 1:
  - − Getting Started
  - − Leading the Change
- ▪ Week 2:
  - − Week in the Classroom
  - − Kicking it Up a Notch

Two or three presentations were published in each strand each day, Monday through Friday, so four to six new presentations were made available each day over the course of the two weeks. The week prior to the conference, a preconference keynote was posted. Again, this was a prerecorded webcast with various opportunities for asynchronous discussion.

All presentations were archived online for posterity along with presentations from previous years. Opportunities for live interaction were scheduled on the Saturday following the pre-conference keynote and the Saturdays following each week of the regular conference. These "fireside chats" were hosted with the support of EdTechTalk. The live sessions utilized two different technologies: an *Ustream* channel video webcast/broadcast of the live presentation, and an interactive, text-based chat room for "backchannel" discussions among participants as well as presenters. During the "Fireside chat," episode hosts as well as a conference presenter introduced a session and then played back all or a portion of that session over *Ustream.* Following the presentation, hosts as well as backchannel participants engaged in a Q&A dialog with the presenter.

Looking at this conference from an organizational perspective, we can see that this organizational model provides participants with a great deal of control by supporting interaction in a variety of mediums and offering participants a high level of flexibility. A breakdown of the interaction and flexibility afforded by this model is provided in Figures 5.4 and 5.5. Each

Indications of Supported Interaction:	High vs. Low Interaction Supported	K12 Online Conference
Time given for interaction during synchronous events?	High	Synchronous events featured a short webcast followed by approximately one hour of text chat between participants, hosts, and presenters.
Is social interaction supported? How?	Medium	Yes, participants are encouraged to introduce themselves in a "Getting to know you" forum. Also, the organizers have started groups which participants can join in order to interact and collaborate. Participants may also start their own groups. The Ning site also encourages participants to create a profile site allowing others to learn of common interests, location, hobbies, et cetera. No synchronous social events were supported.
Is asynchronous (presentation-related) interaction supported?	High	Yes, there is a blog space set up for each of the individual presentations as well as asynchronous discussion forums for each of the strands. In addition, participants can comment on presentations below the posted videos.
Are trained moderators provided for synchronous and/or asynchronous discussions?	High	Moderators are present in both the synchronous events and asynchronous forums.
Are Web 2.0 applications employed? How so?	High	Yes, the conference site includes a widget for social bookmarks, a conference tag, a Twitter hashtag, and a Facebook page. The home page of the conference blog included links to aggregators such as Technorati. In addition, the conference Ning included a Frappr map through which the physical location of participants can be visualized.

Figure 5.4 Support of interaction.

Flexibility Afforded:	High vs. Low Flexibility for Participants	K12 Online Conference
Are presentations synchronous and/or asynchronous?	High	All of the presentations are asynchronous. However, some of the recorded webcasts are re-presented during synchronous sessions.
Are live presentations recorded and archived?	High	Yes.
Are synchronous presentations available at various times around the clock?	Low	No, synchronous presentations are offered on Saturdays between 1pm and 6pm GMT only.
Are multiple real-time presentations scheduled simultaneously?	High	No, synchronous presentations are scheduled at different times.
What types of communication mediums are available to participants?	Medium	Asynchronous presentations used recorded audio or video webcasts. Synchronous and asynchronous interaction is done via text only.
Are Web 2.0 applications and aggregators employed so that flexibility is promoted?	High	Yes, the conference provided tags, Facebook group, and a link to Technorati.

Figure 5.5 Support of flexibility.

indication of interaction is rated as high, medium, or low, relative to other conferences that we have studied and/or in which we have participated.

Dual-Mode Conferences

Dual mode conferences, sometimes referred to as *blended* or *hybrid* conferences, combine an f2f conference with an online conference. This organizational model originated as a means of improving accessibility and expanding the global reach of established f2f conferences. In the past, conference presentations were conveyed via text and/or television, and interaction was supported via email. Today's technologies enable streaming of live events to an online audience. Interaction between the presenters and online participants during live presentations may be supported by an on-site moderator who relays questions and comments from the online participants to the presenter and on-site participants. Dual-mode conferences can also provide temporal flexibility through the use of recorded presentations. Recordings of live events can be archived on the conference Web site and retrieved in multimedia formats. Asynchronous interaction between the online participants and the presenter may be encouraged in discussion forums and blogs after the live presentation.

Case Study of a Dual-Mode Conference:

Cardiff Online: http://iatefl.britishcouncil.org/2009/

Cardiff Online provided online coverage of the 43rd Annual International Association of Teachers of English as a Foreign Language (IATEFL) Conference, which took place in Cardiff, Wales. The online conference was offered free of charge, while the f2f conference cost between £95 (student IATEFL members) and £200 (non-members). The Cardiff Online Web site provided online participants with information on every presentation taking place in Cardiff. All of the session description pages included links to support materials, such as presenter Web sites, blogs, and the PowerPoint presentations. Many of the sessions were streamed live to the online audience. These presentations were recorded, and both audio and video recordings were posted to the conference Web site. These recordings will remain available to the online community indefinitely. The online conference did not offer synchronous interaction. However, participants were encouraged to join the asynchronous discussion forums related to the sessions.

Cardiff Online attempted to build connections between the live conference and the online participants in a number of ways. First, the conference organizers sponsored two roving reporters. These reporters attended the live conference and blogged continuously about their experiences. Online participants were able to respond to the blog posts. Second, the Cardiff Online Web site provided a *Twitter* feed that included tweets from both live and online participants. Finally, online participants were encouraged to pose questions for live interviews with some of the conference presenters. These interviews were then streamed live to the online participants and the recording of the interview was posted to the conference Web site. The conference Web site (http://iatefl.britishcouncil.org/2009/) was used to aggregate blog and *Twitter* posts, display conference photos, provide links to recorded sessions, and note topics and links to asynchronous text discussions. These additional communication channels were used by both the online and f2f participants to organize and maximize interaction opportunities.

Emerging Trends

Dual-Mode Conferences in Reverse

Ten years ago, Shimabukuro (2000) predicted that the focus of dual-mode conferences would shift from the live event to the online event, "*f2f within Virtual.*" In this model, f2f events are integrated into an online conference. The superstructure is based in the Internet, and built into it are pockets of f2f interaction where individuals benefit from both interactions: local f2f and global virtual (Shimabukuro, 2000). The economic issues and environmental awareness that have arisen in recent years have acted as catalysts for this shift. More often, we are seeing f2f meetings supplementing online conferences. The Virtual Conference on Climate Change and CO2 Storage provides an example of this organizational model. The conference took place in December, 2008 and was an experimental one-day conference consisting of three presenters and multiple poster sessions. The presentations took place in *Second Life* and were attended by participants from around the world. In addition, each presentation was broadcast live in conference rooms at Imperial College, Stanford University, University of Wyoming, University of Southern California, and University of Texas at Austin. Interaction between and amongst presenters and participants in all venues was facilitated by on-site moderators. This type of distributed presentation was popular twenty years ago when satellite television was used to beam a famous speaker to rooms distributed throughout a continent. The increased personal and room-based multi-way communications tools now available create opportunities for groups at one location to interact with other groups and the presenters, in addition to interaction at the f2f level in the local venue.

Unconferences

Recognizing the expertise possessed by conference participants and the value of shared knowledge, some organizations have adopted radically different formats that capitalize on the experience of participants. These new formats fall under the umbrella moniker *unconference.* "An unconference is a facilitated, participant-driven conference centered around a theme or purpose" (Unconference, 2009). The term *unconference* has been applied to a wide range of gatherings, including barcamps, Foo Camps, and Knowledge Cafés. These events take advantage of the knowledge, skill, and understanding possessed by conference participants by allowing them to decide the session topics, set the agenda, and learn from each other in a cooperative and informal setting. Unconference sessions have been praised as a refreshing approach to getting participants involved in presenting and discussing topics that are timely and relevant to everyone in attendance (Darby, 2009; Fernandez, 2007).

Unconferences require very little advance planning, as the agenda is developed by the participants. However, unconference organizers warn that it is imperative to have someone facilitating the event who understands both the structure and the audience (Fernandez, 2007). Unconferences may be organized as stand-alone events, or as a component of a larger traditional conference. Most unconferences utilize an "open grid approach" whereby a blank grid is used for scheduling. The grid identifies rooms on the horizontal axis and times on the vertical axis. The unconference commences with a brainstorming session where participants are asked to suggest topics of interest. They may also volunteer to present topics or facilitate discussions. The participants then vote to decide which topics will be included in the schedule. As topics are decided upon, they're placed on the grid, along with the names of presenters or facilitators. Participants are then free to attend the sessions of interest to them.

Structuring the Unconference

Fernandez (2007) provides the following tips, from unconference veterans Leahy & Associates, for structuring an unconference.

- In order to keep the content focussed, identify a subject for the unconference.
- Provide thorough information to all participants, explaining the unconference concept and structure so that they know what to expect. "Explain that they'll be asked to participate, either by suggesting topics or volunteering to present or facilitate a discussion" (Fernandez, 2007). Participants may also be asked to blog or Twitter about the event.
- Make sure that registrants understand that the unconference sessions are selected by the participants.
- Establish unconference rules that reinforce the need to show respect for other participants' opinions. Inform participants that those who are disrespectful will be asked to leave.
- Identify the types of sessions that will be included (e.g., presentations, workshops, discussions).
- Make clear to participants that they may leave a session if it is not meeting their expectations.
- "Ask participants to arrive with an open mind and trust the process" (Fernandez, 2007, p. 57).

This organizational model has seen growing application in online conferences. In the online environment, the brainstorming session is an asynchronous event that takes place over several weeks prior to the unconference. Wikis and discussion boards are frequently used for this purpose. Once the sessions have been agreed upon, they are posted to a schedule. As in f2f conferences, schedules are often represented by an open grid; however, locations on the horizontal axis are represented by URLs to synchronous conferencing platforms or locations within *Second Life*. Examples of online unconferences include the following:

- Jokaydia Unconference (http://jokaydia.wikispaces.com/unconference09): a weekend unconference taking place on the Islands of Jokaydia in *Second Life*. "The Jokaydia Unconference is a free event which provides professional development and networking opportunities for educators and facilitators who are exploring innovative strategies, spaces and technologies for learning. The aim of [the] annual Unconference is to celebrate the year's discoveries and achievements and welcome SL residents both old and new to share their work ... and you are invited to participate! Propose a presentation, workshop, roleplay, game or panel session." The Jokaydia Unconference also included an f2f portion that was integrated into the online event.
- OPALescence 2009 (http://opalescence.wetpaint.com/): a free, two-day, online library conference combining a traditional speaker schedule with an unconference portion. Both the speaker sessions and the unconference sessions were held in a live Web conferencing platform where participants could interact via VoIP and text chatting.

Design Considerations

As seen from the examples provided in this chapter, there are a multitude of organizational models available for the design of an online conference. So how does one decide on the model to use? What factors need to be considered? What elements must be included?

The first and most important factor to consider in the design of an online conference is the participants (Wieman, 2001). The characteristics and needs of the participants influence all other elements of the design. Figure 5.6 provides a conceptual model of the design factors for an online conference. This model and the following component descriptions were adapted from Wieman's (2001) conceptual model of a virtual conference.

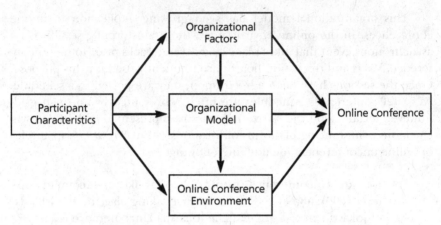

Figure 5.6 Conceptual model of the design factors for an online conference. Adapted from Weiman, 2001.

Participant Characteristics

Online conference participants are usually adult learners who are dedicating time and expending money on the conference. Consequently, if the conference does not fulfill their personal and professional needs, they will likely cease to participate (Knowles, 1980; Schon, 1983). An understanding of the participant characteristics is critical to designing an online conference that fulfills those needs. Weiman (2001) listed the following participant characteristics as influential to the outcome of online conferences:

- Expectations: Studies of computer-mediated communication have demonstrated that pre-expectations become self-fulfilling prophecies. Thus, if participants have high expectations of the online conference, they will be more likely to dedicate time and effort to making it successful.
- Skills and experience: This refers to the skills necessary to operate the technologies and interact online. Besides raw technical skill, a sense of self-efficacy in regard to communications tools is also associated with successful operation efficacy (Eastin & LaRose, 2000)
- Feelings of Community: This characteristic is born from previous experience with the conference community. It is argued that participants who feel part of that community will be more likely to show commitment to the group and be more comfortable interacting with community members.

- Motivation: Motivation to learn has been identified by many adult learning researchers as a major factor influencing both participation in CPE activities and subsequent application of learning in the workplace (Axtell & Maitlis, 1997; Mathieu, Tannenbaum, & Salas, 1992). Motivation is in turn influenced by personal and professional relevance, personal energy, feelings of wellbeing, and feelings of confidence and competence.
- Attitude: Participants come to an online conference possessing attitudinal traits that may either foster or inhibit their participation in the online conference. In a study of students taking online courses, Hiltz (1994) found that students with more positive pre-course attitudes toward computers and the specific platform being used were more likely to participate actively online and to perceive greater benefits from the online classroom mode. Likewise, conference participants with more positive attitudes toward the software being utilized may be more likely to interact in that particular mode (i.e., *Twitter*, blogs, synchronous conferencing software, etc.).
- Culture: One of the advantages of online conferences is that it facilitates interaction between global participants. Consequently, participants may come from a variety of cultures with varying social norms. But, as importantly, online culture is new to many participants and developing the skills and attitudes that allow one to operate effectively online takes time and attention to the online context
- Language: Due to the global nature of online conferences, participants may communicate in different languages, but as in f2f encounters globally, the predominant language used is English.
- Technology: This characteristic refers to the technologies and bandwidth that are accessible to the participants.
- Time: The time available to participation in an online conference is affected by work, family, and distance (due to time zone differences).

The last two characteristics, *technology* and *time*, should be thought of not only as design considerations but as requirements of the participants. It would be impossible to design an online conference without some requirements of technology and time from the participants. These requirements should be stated prior to participant registration in order to avoid frustration or disillusionment.

We would like to add *physical disabilities* to the characteristics provided by Weiman (2001). Many participants possess physical disabilities that need to be considered in the design of the conference. Following guidelines and recommendations for universal accessibility is becoming increasingly important and is especially so for organizers of online conferences, who are attempting to attract participants with a variety of physical challenges. Conference organizers must go beyond the one-way focus of most Web site developers to insure that contributions of online conference participants are also accessible to all users (Jaeger & Xie, 2009).

Although it may be difficult to address all of these characteristics, an understanding of participant characteristics can be a valuable source of information in the planning of the conference. For example, knowing that the participants are more likely to interact if they feel part of the community, organizers would be well advised to organize activities that build community prior to or early in the conference. They may also want to incorporate software that supports the community within and outside of the conference parameters.

Organizational Factors

The organizational factors are influenced by the participant characteristics, and in turn, directly affect the design of the virtual conference. These factors are:

- Objectives: Beyond learning specific content and keeping abreast of new developments, the objectives of an online CPE conference often include opportunities for collaboration, decision-making, and networking.
- Content: It is critical that the subjects covered in the conference are relevant to the participants' situations. Anderson and Christiansen (2004) implore online conference organizers to "stress themes, presentations, and activities that are timely and tuned to the emerging needs of prospective participants" (p. 22). The range of topics covered will also influence the organizational model. Allowing opportunities for participants to shape the conference (have some unconference capabilities) by selecting topics for roundtable or breakout sessions, for example, serves to increase the relevancy of the online conference
- Time: The time frame provided for the conference must be long enough to cover the content and allow for interaction, while being short enough to sustain the attention of the participants. This

time frame may limit the number and types of activities that may be included.

- ▪ Size: Attendance numbers of an online conference are not restricted by venue capacity as in a f2f conference. However, the expected attendance will have some bearing on the number of sessions planned, the platforms to be used, and the types of interaction incorporated.

Conclusion

The participant characteristics and the organizational factors described above inform the decisions that conference organizers must make in regards to the activities to include, the scheduling of events, the types of technology to employ, and the personnel needed to make a conference work. In addition, conference organizers must decide how much control will be afforded to the participants in the way of interaction and flexibility. For those just beginning to consider organizing an online conference, this may seem an overwhelming task.

In the remaining chapters, we endeavor to assist online conference organizers by providing additional examples of organizational formats used in online conferences and information on support available for both the organization and delivery of online conferences. In addition, and central to this book, is the information gleaned from interviews with experienced online conference organizers. Transcripts of the interviews were analyzed for emergent themes leading to suggestions and guidelines that conference organizers could follow to gain maximum value and increase efficiency of this mode of professional development.

6

Online Conference Evaluation

Introduction

Participation in traditional professional conferences poses a burden both financially and personally on professionals who are required to leave their work and families. This burden is shared with employers who provide the financing necessary for employee attendance at these conferences and support their temporary absence from the workplace. Yet, there is a shocking lack of evidence for the effectiveness of professional conferences. As stated in Chapter 1, the overarching goal of continuing professional education (CPE) has been described as the establishment, maintenance, and improvement of professional knowledge, skills, and attitude resulting in improved performance (Cervero, 2001; Knox, 2000; Mott, 2000). In line with this goal, the objectives of CPE conferences (simply put) are considered to be knowledge creation and networking that result in improvements in professional practice. Most online conferences also promote the establishment of communities of practice with an assumption that these connections also lead to increased professional competence and capacity. However, evaluations of conferences rarely determine whether these objectives have been achieved. Most evaluations of professional conferences, whether face-to-

Online Conferences: Professional Development for a Networked Era, pages 73–85
Copyright © 2010 by Information Age Publishing
All rights of reproduction in any form reserved.

face (f2f) or online, are generally concerned only with the immediate reactions of participants (e.g., *Were the speakers interesting? How was the registration process?*). As importantly for transferable knowledge gained, the results of these evaluations are rarely made public and thus are not accessible for further study.

The root of this problem may be seen in the lack of incentives and scholarly attention given to the evaluation of professional conferences. Very little has been written about models or approaches to the evaluation of f2f professional conferences, and we find nothing in the literature dealing with evaluation of online professional conferences. What little has been written concerning evaluation of f2f conferences mostly laments the lack of quality evaluation of the status quo and occasionally proposes new models for the evaluation of professional conferences. In this chapter, we hope to make a small step toward addressing this void. We provide a brief review of evaluation theory, examine the limitations of current evaluation practices, describe emerging models, and discuss how these models may be implemented within an online CPE conference.

Evaluation Theory

Early in the development of evaluation as both a practical and academic discipline, Scriven (1967) broadly described evaluation as judging the worth or merit of something. The "something" has come to include a long list of interests, including programs, products, personnel, policy, performance, proposals, and technology (American Evaluation Association, 2004). The most relevant of these areas of interest to ourselves is program evaluation, which encompasses the evaluation of educational and training programs. Fitzpatrick, Sanders, and Worthen (2004) defined formal program evaluation as "the identification, clarification and application of defensible criteria to determine an evaluation object's value (worth or merit) in relation to those criteria" (p. 5). Program evaluation may be further defined by its intended purpose: formative or summative. An evaluation is considered to be formative if the primary purpose is to provide information for program improvement, while summative evaluations provide information to assist in making decisions regarding such things as program adoption, continuation or expansion (Fitzpatrick et al., 2004).

Theories and models of best program evaluation offer diverse views, which have led to alternative approaches. Fitzpatrick et al. (2004) have grouped the various evaluation approaches into five categories: objectives-oriented, management-oriented, consumer-oriented, expertise-oriented, and participant-oriented. They do not promote one approach over another, but rather assert that "each of the evaluation frameworks offers a different perspective on evaluation that can be applied to some, but not all evaluation situations" (p. 165). The decision as to which approach to use is often based on evaluator and client preferences, as "there is almost no research to guide one's choice" (p. 156). However, they recommend careful consideration of the purpose of the evaluation, the intended audience of the evaluation and the resources available for the evaluation. In addition, they warn evaluators against uncritical adherence to any one particular approach. They promote instead an eclectic approach whereby the evaluator chooses and combines concepts from different evaluation approaches as they seem appropriate (Fitzpatrick et al., 2004). This, of course, requires that the evaluator be familiar with a variety of approaches.

The difficulty of knowing which evaluation approach to use is compounded when the evaluation takes place online. In an article focused on the evaluation of e-Learning programs, Mungania and Hatcher (2004) point out that there are many more factors affecting online learners than f2f learners, as they must "interact synchronously or asynchronously with the instructor, other learners, technology and virtual learning communities" (p. 34). A similar comparison may be made between f2f conference participants and online conference participants, as the latter must interact synchronously or asynchronously with a variety of distributed others through a mediated, technological interface. In addition to the multiple factors affecting online conference participation, evaluators of online professional conferences must overcome the challenge of gathering data from conference organizers, presenters, and participants who are geographically dispersed.

Current Evaluation Practices

Conference evaluation typically entails completing questionnaires at the end of individual sessions and/or at the conclusion of the conference. Online conference evaluation questionnaires are implemented using online survey or quiz tools. The link to the evaluation is emailed to participants and posted to the conference Web site. Some synchronous conferencing platforms also provide an evaluation feature that automatically pops open a questionnaire when participants leave the live online session. Evaluation questionnaires usually investigate participant reactions to various aspects of the conference and perceptions of value and learning. For example, most online conference questionnaires include inquiries about the following:

- Relevance of topics/sessions
- Quality/effectiveness of sessions

- Level of attendee participation in the online conference
- Technical difficulties experienced
- Availability and effectiveness of technical support
- Features, media, and tools used by participants
- Suggestions for improvements for future online conferences
- Perceived worth and benefit of the conference
- Perceived value of new knowledge gained through participation in the conference

Most evaluation surveys solicit structured responses and provide predominantly quantitative results. Item types used in evaluation surveys include: multiple choice items; adjectival responses (responses are made on a five-point scale ranging from *excellent* to *poor*); Likert Scale items (respondents indicate their level of agreement/disagreement with a statement); adverb responses (responses are made on a five-point scale ranging from *always* to *never*); and short-answer, open-ended questions for which content analysis is used to count emergent themes or highest mentioned issues (Fitzpatrick et al., 2004).

This type of evaluation has been criticized for presenting a shallow illustration of the value or worth of a CPE event. It relies on participant perceptions and does not determine if the intended goals of the event were achieved (Furze & Pearcey, 1999; Chapman, Wiessner, Storberg-Walker, & Hatcher, 2007). This approach to conference evaluation is reflective of the first of Kirkpatrick's four levels for the evaluation of training. The model was first proposed in 1959 and has received enduring attention in training evaluation literature since (Kirkpatrick, 2010). The complete model consists of four levels of questions (though a fifth level for evaluating return on investment [ROI] was proposed by Phillips [1997]):

1. Reaction: How do participants feel about the program?
2. Learning: What did the participants learn in the program?
3. Behavior: Did participant behavior change as a result of attending the program?
4. Results: What organizational benefits resulted from this change in behavior? (Kirkpatrick, 1977)

Reaction questions (Level 1) are used to determine how the learner (participant) feels about various aspects of the training intervention (conference). Reaction questions may also seek information from the subjects about their perception of the other levels, for example, whether they achieved their learning objectives (learning level) or how they think the training will change their future behavior. However, "a personal reaction to the learning experience may or may not correspond with other external measures of the impact of the learning experience" (Belanger & Jordan, 2000, p. 191). Although it is important to gage levels of participant satisfaction with the conference, relying on participant perceptions as the sole indicator of value is inadequate.

Unfortunately, despite their overall appeal, the second, third, and fourth levels have not been widely used due to their perceived complexity (Kaufmann, Keller, & Watkins, 1995) and the difficulty of measuring these levels accurately and inexpensively. In order for evaluators to adequately assess the second, third, and fourth levels of impact, they must gather information from the learners, their colleagues, and/or their supervisors prior to and long after the training event. Observation of the subject's behavior prior to and after the training is also recommended (Kirkpatrick, 1998). The complexity of implementing all four of Kirkpatrick's levels increases drastically when one considers applying it to the evaluation of an online conference where participants hail from different organizations and are geographically dispersed.

In addition to the issue of complexity, there is the question of validity when Kirkpatrick's third- and fourth-level questions are applied to the evaluation of a professional conference. The value of a professional conference cannot be judged on the evidence of participant behavior changes alone, as many other factors influence the uptake of behavior change and the potential organizational benefits. As Cervero (1985) has argued, an organization or social system that is not supportive of change will be unlikely to encourage the professional to change behavior. Insufficient funds or materials, lack of support from supervisors, and/or lack of cooperation from colleagues may also deter the most motivated of professionals from implementing new ideas or procedures in their workplaces (Meyer, 2007). Finally, critics have noted that the Kirkpatrick model focuses heavily on outcomes and "doesn't take into account the process leading to the results" (Bernthal, 1995, p. 43). The questions do not ask "how" or "why" the results occurred. For example, if used to evaluate an online conference, the questions would not directly address the reasons *why* learning and networking did or did not take place. Bernthal (1995) argues that Kirkpatrick's four levels have "limited our thinking regarding evaluation and possibly hindered our ability to conduct meaningful evaluation" (Bernthal, 1995, p. 41).

Clearly, Kirkpatrick's four-level approach is not an appropriate choice for the evaluation of a professional conference, nor was it intended to be used for this purpose. While first-level reaction questions may elicit valuable information for conference evaluators, they do not provide sufficient measure alone. Although there are many alternative approaches that could be applied to the evaluation of a professional conference, there are very few examples of organizers who have actually gone beyond traditional end-of-conference survey forms. The following two case studies are the only examples we were able to find where alternative approaches to the evaluation of an f2f professional conference were used. However, we believe that these alternative approaches could be carried out more easily and perhaps more effectively in an online conference.

New Evaluation Methods

Responsive Evaluation

In 1999, Spiegel, Bruning, and Giddings experimented with using an alternative approach to evaluating an f2f professional conference. They chose to conduct a "responsive evaluation" of the conference. This participant-oriented approach was developed by Stake (1975, 1976, 1985), who defined an evaluation as responsive "if it orients more directly to program activities than to program intents; responds to audience requirements for information; and if the different value perspectives present are referred to in reporting the success and failure of the program" (1975, p. 14). In this case, "value perspectives" refers to the numerous and often different goals and outcomes expected by organizers, participants, funders, and others. Responsive evaluation requires evaluators to continuously interact with members of various stakeholder groups to determine what information they desire and the manner in which they prefer to receive such information (Fitzpatrick et al., 2004). "Responsive evaluators are relatively disinterested in formal objectives or the precision of formalized data collection; they are more likely to be at home working within the naturalistic or ethnographic paradigm, drawing heavily on qualitative techniques" (Fitzpatrick et al., 2004, p. 137).

In applying this approach to the evaluation of an f2f conference, Spiegel et al. (1999) hoped not only to determine the value of the conference, but also to make the evaluation an integral part of the conference itself. They point out that,

> In spite of conference participants being primary beneficiaries of a conference, they are rarely asked to participate in conducting conference evaluations, aside from filling out summative evaluation forms. And seldom are they considered to be primary evaluation audiences. The responsive model

we used allowed participants to contribute interactively in the evaluation process. (pp. 63–66)

The methods used in this example of responsive evaluation are briefly described here:

- Interviews: Interviews began at the initial registration and continued during break times throughout the conference. Interviewees were chosen randomly and asked two or three prepared questions. Participant comments were printed onto overheads and prominently displayed in the lobby of the conference center.
- Reaction/feedback forms: Representative comments from the interviews were selected, compiled, and reproduced on forms. These were distributed to all participants, who were then asked to react to and comment on the statements in a space provided on the form. Individual reaction forms were made available to participants for viewing and displayed using the overhead projector in the lobby. This method was intended to promote interaction between the conference participants and the evaluation process. Unfortunately, Spiegel et al. (1999) did not discuss the issue of anonymity in their study; however, we assume that the confidentiality of participants was protected.
- Photographs: Photos of speakers, participants, handouts, display areas, and other conference activities were displayed on a board in the lobby. The intention was to provide detailed reminders to participants about the level of activity and participation in different sessions, the variety of activities occurring at the conference, and the reaction of participants to different aspects of their experiences.
- Summative evaluation form: A summative evaluation form was distributed at the conclusion of the conference. In addition to inquiring about the overall quality of the conference, this form asked participants to provide ratings of their own effort, emphasizing the role that participants play in the success of a conference and (in this case) in the evaluation.
- Presentation of results: In the final plenary session of the conference, the evaluators summarized the conference evaluation for the participants and presented a qualitative analysis of the results gathered by the different evaluation methods used during the conference.

Results and Discussion

By applying a responsive approach to evaluation of a professional CPE conference, the Spiegel et al. (1999) allowed evaluators to participate actively in the conference and encouraged participants to be involved in and assume some ownership of the evaluation. As expected, participants represented diverse groups with differing needs and purposes for attending the conference. "The responsive evaluation gathered information from and responded to information requirements from all of these participant groups, recognizing and validating their different perspectives by including their feedback" (Spiegel et al., 1999, p. 63). In addition, the interactive nature of the evaluation not only provided information for the evaluators, but it also prompted informal discussion among participants. "In a manner somewhat analogous to the often-rich discussions that occur at conferences in hotel lobbies, hallways, and restaurants, the display of comments and then others' reactions to the comments seemed to create a kind of 'conversation' about the intellectual agenda of the conference" (Spiegel et al., 1999, p. 66).

Other benefits attributed to the responsive evaluation were:

- Provides a richer and more detailed interpretation of the successes and failures of the conference.
- The responsive nature of the evaluation can mitigate biases introduced by the impersonal, quantitative, post-conference nature of traditional evaluations.
- Provides the audience with pertinent and timely feedback. (Spiegel et al., 1999)

The evaluators of this conference offered two cautions regarding the use of responsive evaluation in conferences. First, because of the interactive nature of this approach, there is a risk of creating a "snowball" effect, where the tone of initial comments may set the tone for the entire evaluation. Positive comments influence a more positive perspective by participants and negative comments lead to a more negative perspective. Second, the constant interactive feedback may become overwhelming for both the participants and the evaluators. "Since the lines between what is being evaluated and the evaluation itself become blurred, interpretation is more difficult and the instruments may become redundant" (Spiegel et al., 1999, p. 66).

Responsive Evaluation in an Online Professional Conference

The responsive evaluation approach used in this pilot study was characterized by the "use of ongoing, interactive communication between the evaluators and the participants, the attention the evaluators pay to the conference participants and their perspectives, the qualitative nature of the information gathered, and the integration of the evaluation into the conference" (Spiegel et al., 1999, p. 58). However, one of the limitations of this approach is that it requires a large time-commitment from highly skilled evaluators (Hurteau & Nadeau, 1985; Klintberg, 1976; Stake, 1985). One of the greatest advantages of online professional conferences has been identified as the affordance of ongoing interactive communication. This affordance makes the responsive approach well suited to the evaluation of an online CPE conference, and in fact, the methods used in this pilot study could easily, and perhaps more effectively, be employed within an online conference. For example, in the study, the interview questions and subsequent responses were handwritten by participants, then compiled into a data file by evaluators and printed onto overheads. In addition, hard copies of the interviews and responses were printed and distributed. This process was time-consuming and not particularly environmentally friendly. In an online conference, the interviews could be conducted by email, phone, Web conferencing, or a survey tool. Interview comments could easily be copied, aggregated as needed, and posted to the conference Web site or any Web 2.0 application used as part of the conference. Participants could be provided with a link to a survey tool that would then allow them to respond to the interview comments anonymously or optionally through identification by their names. Evaluation and ratings of particular session could be revealed to participants in real time so that they could compare their reactions and assessments to others and to group means, thereby generating motivation and interest in completing activity evaluations. Once again, responses could be copied and pasted to the conference Web site. An alternative method available to online conference evaluators would be to post the interview questions in an evaluation forum or blog where responses could be posted and commented on by all participants. This method requires a strategy for allowing for both confidentiality and exposure of participants, dependent upon their choices.

Not only does the online venue provide a medium that is conducive to interaction, it enables this interaction to be shared with all stakeholders and recorded for further evaluation purposes. In addition, the online conference provides a podium and a persistent archive for the perspectives of the conference participants that is integrated into the conference platform and proceedings. All of these affordances support the goals of responsive evaluation.

A second alternative approach to the evaluation of a professional conference used a similar technique to synthesize evaluation with active learning. The evaluators dubbed it *New Learning.*

New Learning

New Learning (NL) was proposed by Chapman et al. (2007) as an alternative way of looking at conference evaluation. They describe it as "the next generation" of evaluation. Initially, NL was developed in an attempt to facilitate knowledge creation within professional conferences. The approach was first applied in the Academy of Human Resources (AHRD) 2005 International Research Conference (an f2f conference). During this case study, the researchers realized that the approach also served to address two common criticisms of traditional conference evaluation:

1. Most conference evaluations focus on participant satisfaction and reactions to the event. They do not evaluate the learning that actually occurs.
2. The quantitative methods used in most conferences to gather and report evaluation results do not capture many of the benefits and limitations of conferences as experienced by conference participants (Chapman et al. 2007, pp. 261–262).

The first of these concerns mirrors the criticism of program evaluations that focus only on easily gathered reaction data at Kirkpatrick's first level of evaluation. The second critique is illustrated when results of participants' evaluation are returned to presenters and organizers. Exactly what does a mean rating of 3.7 on a 5-point satisfaction scale mean? By contrast, Chapman et al. found that the NL approach not only contributed to knowledge creation within the conference, it also provided valuable qualitative evaluation feedback to stakeholders.

The methods used in the AHRD (2005) Research Conference included pre-conference communications to attendees describing the theoretical foundations and rationale for embedding NL in the conference. The primary method used to collect data was the *New Learning Data Forms.* These were included in registration packages and made available on tables at all scheduled conference sessions. The forms included a reflective question that "prompted attendees to provide deeper information than typical evaluations: *'Please tell us about any new learning you have experienced or any new questions that have occurred to you as a result of the conference?'*" (Chapman et al., 2007, p. 265). The participants were also asked to identify the nature of the new learning (formal or informal) and the setting in which it occurred:

a specific session, in the hallway, or over dinner. The researchers noted that many of the attendees seemed to value this part of the procedure, as it provided an impetus and structured time for them to reflect on and write about their conference experiences (Chapman et al., 2007). The conference organizers and NL researchers also promoted the NL approach during the conference through banners, flyers, tote bags, and staff t-shirts.

Results and Discussion

In order to track submissions and determine participation, attendees were given a randomly assigned number to place at the top of the NL data forms. This number ensured anonymity and also served to encourage participation, as completion of forms qualified participants for daily prize drawings. Participants' unique numbers served as a ticket for that purpose. In addition to the forms, data was gathered from interviews with selected participants and semi-structured observations by the evaluation team. The NL evaluators analyzed all of the data for themes that emerged repeatedly. In all, seven such themes surfaced. Findings from this conference study were reported in newsletters, journal articles, and subsequent conferences so that the data was widely available to HRD scholars, practitioners, and other interested groups or individuals. Making this data available to stakeholders is considered a critical component of the NL approach, as it provides divergent perspectives and experiences of conference attendees and may benefit future work (Chapman et al., 2007).

Chapman et al. (2007) point out that NL is ideally suited to professional conferences where learning is an explicit goal.

> Not only can NL assess congruence of intended outcomes with actual outcomes, it extends popular notions of evaluation by changing the learning event itself. NL contributes to knowledge creation, and actually speeds knowledge generation by making what is learned at an event available to a larger audience. NL shortens the time of exposure to new ideas and theories, giving participants, both scholars and practitioners, more dynamic and responsive ways of learning and constructing knowledge. (p. 268)

The researchers are also quick to add that although NL focuses on the participants, the approach can also be used to assist conference planners, as it examines the ways in which the program or event facilitates or hinders learning. Consequently, it allows for the collection of information related to the conference venue, schedule, and organization.

New Learning in an Online Professional Conference

For many of the same reasons stated in the discussion of responsive evaluation, the NL approach appears to be well suited to the evaluation of an online conference. All of the methods used in the AHRD (2005) Research Conference could be transferred, and in many cases enhanced, through online provision. Pre-conference communication regarding the NL approach could be accomplished using email and a pre-conference learning event. Promotion of the approach could be achieved on the conference Web site. The New Learning data forms could be completed using online quiz or survey tools and interviews could be conducted using email, telephone, or Web-conferencing software. Instead of observations, the recordings of live sessions and archived text forums would provide a rich source of data for evaluators. The evaluators of this conference attempted to motivate attendees' participation in the evaluation through use of a raffle drawing from submitted NL forms; this type of incentive for participation could also be used in online conference evaluations.

As stated above, making the evaluation data available to stakeholders is considered a critical component of the NL approach. Distribution of this information could be achieved with less delay and fewer costs online than possible otherwise. Thus, NL used to evaluate an online conference would not only shorten the time before exposure to new ideas and theories, but also reduce the costs of that exposure, while giving participants more dynamic and responsive ways of learning and constructing knowledge.

Conclusion

The evaluation literature regarding evaluation of professional conferences has received little attention, especially as compared to the amount of funding spent on this type of development activity. Likewise, the literature on f2f and online professional conferences offers little to guide evaluators or conference organizers. Evaluations based on participant reactions, despite frequent criticism as to their inadequacy, remain the status quo. Our intent is not to promote any particular approach for the evaluation of an online conference. Rather, we wish to encourage online conference evaluators to venture outside of the box and exploit the affordances of the online environment to enhance the quality, quantity, and relevance of conference evaluations. As demonstrated in this chapter, evaluations of online professional conferences offer opportunities hitherto unavailable to conference organizers. We hope that the theory and case studies presented here will prompt evaluators to take a closer look at this area of conference design and motivate online conference organizers to plan and implement new evaluation approaches that take advantage of the affordances of the online venue.

7

Emergence of Infrastructure and Commercial Support for Online Conferences

Introduction

The first online conferences were organized using rather unsophisticated but accessible tools like email lists and usenet groups. As the technologies became more functional, demand arose for services that could reduce the complexity and workload for conference organizers, while increasing the functionality and services provided to participants. Thus, the mid 1990s witnessed the launch of several private companies offering online conferencing software. Since that time, the rapid development of online technologies and the accessibility of large bandwidth connections have drastically increased the number of delivery tools available, and the online conferencing industry has grown rapidly. Today, there are over 100 commercial providers, including large corporate players such as IBM, Cisco, and Microsoft, now offering online conferencing platforms (Taulli, 2007; Woolley, 2007). However, these online conferencing vendors, "differ in their emphasis on educational versus business applications, features offered, software require-

Online Conferences: Professional Development for a Networked Era, pages 87–100
Copyright © 2010 by Information Age Publishing
All rights of reproduction in any form reserved.

ments, and pricing models" (Shield et al., 2005, S28). In addition, most of these vendors focus on the provision of their platform. They do not provide support in the organization and promotion of large online events with multiple presenters and widely dispersed audiences.

This chapter looks at several companies that are now offering comprehensive services for both the organization and delivery of online continuing professional education (CPE) conferences. These companies provide expertise to corporations, organizations, and associations who would like to host a CPE event online but who lack the experience, tool set, and know-how necessary to organize a successful event. Information on these companies was obtained directly from their Web sites, promotional materials, and interviews with company executives. This list is not exhaustive but is intended to raise awareness of the software and services available to organizations offering to host and facilitate an online conference. No preferences or recommendations are intended by the authors. Convenient links to company Web sites are provided in a table at the end of the chapter.

Commercial Support for the Organization and Delivery of Online Conferences

The commercial enterprises discussed in this chapter not only provide the platform for an online conference, but they also support many of the organizational aspects related to the event. The type of support offered may be categorized as administrative, technical, and pedagogical. These categories of support include the following services:

- Administrative:
  - Assistance with the call for papers
  - Advertising and promotion of the event
  - Event planning and scheduling
  - Processing of participant registration and fees (e-commerce)
  - Creation of conference evaluation survey instruments and database
- Technical:
  - Configuring the conference Web site
    - Branding of the site
    - Incorporation of features and options (e.g., wikis, polls, etc.)
    - Setting user access rights and privileges
    - Creation of necessary discussion boards
    - Establishing security and access levels

- Provision of live (synchronous) platforms
- Creation of presentation recordings
- Conversion of presentations to multiple formats (e.g., Flash, MP3, EPub)
- Technical support to conference organizers, presenters, and participants prior to and during the event
- Pedagogical:
  - Recommendations on the volume of content and format of the conference
  - Consultation with presenters in regards to effective media
  - Presenter/moderator coaching
  - Posting of announcements and upcoming events
  - Guidance for participants

Of course, not all companies offer this complete list of services, nor are they always required. The support provided, and the associated cost, is determined through negotiation with individual clients. The remainder of this chapter examines commercial enterprises (listed alphabetically) that have established themselves over the last decade by assisting in the development and organization of several successful online professional development conferences.

The Consultants-E

The Consultants-E specializes in online learning and teaching in higher and adult education. They help higher education institutions and companies implement instructional technology, design online courses and seminars, and train educators in online teaching and learning. In addition, The Consultants-E offers totally customizable and comprehensive services to organizations wishing to host a professional development conference. They have organized and hosted f2f conferences, online conferences, and dual-mode conferences using a large variety of platforms and technologies, including a group of private islands in *Second Life*. The Consultants-E owns and runs these islands, called EduNation, which are dedicated to education, research, training, and distance and blended learning and development. In EduNation, The Consultants-E provide the conference space, a variety of presentational tools, a *Shoutcast* audio service for the streamed audio, and the possibility of audio and video recordings of sessions. For *Second Life* events, they have their own PHP/MySQL Web interface for registration and tracking, and they couple this with in-world groups for more targeted information.

The Consultants-E offers comprehensive administrative, technological, and pedagogical support for most events. An example of a dual-mode conference organized by The Consultants-E is the International Association of Teachers of English as a Foreign Language (IATEFL) Conference. A description of the 2009 conference that took place in Cardiff, Wales is provided in Chapter 5. In 2008, the f2f conference was held in Exeter, England. The online portion of the IATEFL conference utilized an open-source *Moodle* platform to provide participants with audio and video recordings of selected sessions, live streamed plenaries and events, live chat sessions, and moderated special interest discussion forums. In addition, a pre-conference blog and a photo-gallery were available to online participants (http://exeteronline.britishcouncil.org/). Attendance at the f2f conference each year has been approximately 1,500 delegates. In 2008, the online conference portion, "Exeter Online," had just under 4,000 participants from 112 countries and saw over 3,500 forum postings (Gavin Dudeney, personal communication, April 30, 2008). It should be noted that the Exeter Online conference was offered free of charge, whereas the onsite conference fees ranged from £95 (student IATEFL members) to £210 (non-members, late registration). These fees did not include food or accommodations.

Another example of a dual-mode conference hosted by The Consultants-E is the International Wireless Ready Event (http://wirelessready.nucba.ac.jp/). This IATEFL Learning Technologies SIG Event is a simultaneous "real" and *Second Life* international symposium. The "real" portion of this annual event takes place at Nagoya University of Commerce & Business in Japan. Pre-registration for the live event is JPY 2,000 (approx. $24 CAD) for IATEFL /JALT/PacCALL members, and payment on the day of the event was JPY 3,000 (approx. $36 CAD) for non-members. The live events included two or three keynote speakers and several panel sessions. The event was presented simultaneously in *Second Life* on EduNation II via video streams. The SL event is offered free of charge thanks to a large number of sponsors, including The Consultants-E.

In addition to contracted events, The Consultants-E has hosted its own annual online professional development conference, the SLanguages Conference. This event "brings together practitioners and researchers in the field of language education in *Second Life* for a 24-hour event to celebrate languages and cultures within the 3D virtual world" (Slanguages, 2009). The Consutants-E coordinate every aspect of this event, including determining the themes of the conference and selecting speakers. This event is completely subsidized by The Consultants-E and is offered free of charge.

Pricing

Prices for The Consultants-E services are not available on the Web site. As Gavin Dudeney, the Project Director for Consultants-E, explained, each project is unique and involves various demands and a different team of consultants, technicians, and moderators (G. Dudeney, personal communication, May 1, 2008).

Direct Learn Online Conferencing

Direct Learn Online Conferencing is UK-based and has been organizing and hosting online conferences since 2001. Their clients have included the British Educational Communications and Technology Agency (BECTA) and the Joint Information Systems Committee (JISC). JISC is a UK government funded agency that provides leadership in the innovative use of ICT to support education and research in higher education and further education. They contracted Direct Learn in 2006 to host their first online conference, Innovating e-Learning 2006. The conference was considered a huge success, with 395 participants. Since then, Direct Learn has hosted this conference annually for JISC.

Direct Learn uses a highly configured version of *Web Crossing* as the platform for their conferences. This platform affords a variety of software tools, including:

- Bulletin boards
- Online polls
- Mailing lists
- RSS feeds
- Wiki
- Web logs
- instant messaging
- collaborative document editing
- personal and shared calendars

Recorded audio and video presentations are available from the conference site, as are text papers. However, in recent years, Direct Learn and their clients have increased their use of synchronous technologies by linking to Web-based conferencing platforms such as *Elluminate* and *Wimba*. Beyond hosting the conference on their system, Direct Learn's services include complete administrative, technical, and pedagogical support, as described above. In addition, Direct Learn edits the conference proceedings and includes a complete summary of the discussions. This material is published in paperbacks or e-books and sold from their online store. In some cases, the books are included in the cost of the conference and participants are provided with a copy.

Like The Consultants-E, Direct Learn also hosts its own professional development conferences. The founders of Direct Learn have applied their expertise in the areas of deafness and communication technologies to co-ordinating the Supporting Deaf People online conference, which has run annually since 2001. The initial conference in 2001 attracted approximately 130 participants from 9 different countries. In recent years, the conference has seen between 200–250 delegates from 20 different countries spread over 5 continents. This conference is the only international online conference to focus on the needs of deaf people and the professionals who support them. In the US and Canada, sign language interpreters must complete regular continuing education programs in order to maintain their registration and qualifications as interpreters. Direct Learn is one of the few organizations outside of the US and Canada that can certify that professional development. A nominal participant fee of £50 is charged for this conference.

Direct Learn is responsible for all aspects of the Supporting Deaf People conference, including determining the conference theme, soliciting presenters, and creating the schedule. They ensure that all of the presentations are in a format that is accessible to their deaf participants. In addition, they provide daily summaries of each of the asynchronous discussions. This service is not provided directly to commissioned conferences. However, the founders of Direct Learn understand the value of these summaries and recommend this practice to their clients. As part of their services, they work with conference moderators, coaching them on how to best facilitate interaction within the forums and how to create summaries.

Pricing

According to Direct Learn's Web site, the base cost for a short-term conference (four to five days) is approximately £9,500 (14,800 USD). This includes hosting, configuring, and managing the conference, while providing a full service. This includes:

- Setup of all folders and discussions
- Setup of other options required (e.g., wiki, polls, document revision, blogs, etc.)
- Configuring login options and access rights
- Registering the users
- Providing user guides
- Providing technical support to all participants
- Working with workshop facilitators (provided by you)

- Working with workshop presenters, putting their papers and presentations into a suitable format
- Providing reading weeks for delegates before and after the conference
- Providing guidance for facilitators and presenters on how to work effectively within the online environment
- Providing text transcripts of all discussions after the conference

Depending on the services required, the cost may vary. For example, if the client wants delegate fees processed via Direct Learn's secure online facility, there is a fee of £8 per delegate (if the conference is free to all or some delegates, the charge is £3 per free delegate, and £8 per paying delegate).

iCohere

iCohere is a company that specializes in the creation of online collaborative communities for the purpose of e-Learning and professional development. Their software and consulting services provide support for collaborative online courses, communities of practice, and online conferences and events. Their clients include small and large companies as well as government, educational, and non-profit organizations. Online professional development conferences are just one of the ways in which iCohere's platform and comprehensive consulting services are used.

A recent online professional development conference hosted by iCohere was the American Speech-Language-Hearing Association's (ASHA) 2008 Audiology Conference. This eighteen-day conference featured fourteen presentations and attracted over 200 participants from around the world. All of the presentations in this conference consisted of pre-recorded audio accompanied by a PowerPoint presentation. This type of webcast is often referred to as an online *poster session*. Participants were able to interact with the poster session presenters and other participants within asynchronous discussion forums. Some of the presenters also participated in live scheduled text chats. Numerous opportunities for interaction were also provided throughout the conference through participant-created forums, quick meetings, and messaging.

Another conference hosted by iCohere was the 2008 Global Social Responsibility Summit. This conference was co-created with the American Society of Association Executives (ASAE) and The Centre for Association Leadership. This professional development conference provided Certified Association Executive (CAE) credits to participants and was a launching point for global initiatives toward social responsibility. The conference was a dual-mode conference that connected participants at the f2f venue in Washington, DC to hundreds of online participants from around the world in real time using streaming video, streaming audio, two-way conference calling, and chat sessions. Teams at remote sites worked on projects that were then re-presented to participants at other virtual sites and at the f2f conference.

The iCohere platform is highly configurable and supports multiple languages, including English, French, Spanish, and Portugese. iCohere assists organizations in tailoring the site to the goals of their conference by assisting with conference planning prior to the event and providing consultation throughout the conference. iCohere is available either as a fully-managed and secure hosted Internet service or as a software package that may be installed on an organization's server. The iCohere Web site can be set up to include any combination of the following components for communication and collaboration:

- Welcome page: Allows site admin to provide orientation and instructions to new members
  - May add logo
  - Provide a streaming PowerPoint site tour and instructions, or
  - Create a custom welcome presentation with narration
- Announcements: Community bulletin board
  - Send information to all site members or to designated groups
    - Forward to external email
    - Attach files and Web site links
    - Embed images and make them clickable
    - Create multiple-choice polls and RSVPs
- Presentation theatre: Articulate software
  - PowerPoint presentations, in conjunction with a teleconference
  - Live text chat
  - Document sharing.
  - Unlimited number of participants
- Collaboration Meeting Room (20 seat limit)
  - VoIP
  - Video streaming
  - Application sharing
  - PowerPoint animations
  - Session recording
- Discussion forums
  - Create multiple public or private discussion areas and topics
    - Attach files and links

- Archive and restore topic areas
- Search content
- Using listserv, email discussion posts individually or as digests

▪ Web forms
  - Build an unlimited number of custom forms for capturing and sharing information
    - May be used for surveys and evaluation
    - May be exported to MS Excel

▪ Shared calendar: scheduling and coordinating tool
  - Can create shared or private entries
  - Calendar items may be automatically posted as announcements and forwarded to members' external email

▪ Real-time, text-based chat rooms for scheduled meetings

▪ Document library: create a simple document repository

▪ Quick meetings: spontaneous, real-time chat between members

▪ Project management: organize and track tasks

▪ Messages: internal email with external forwarding

▪ Web links: organizes important Web site links

▪ Member directory

▪ Help desk

▪ Preferences: may customize individual site settings

▪ Site search

▪ Custom menu items

In addition, iCohere will provide the following services and features:

▪ Assistance with the creation of Web-based tests and quizzes to support online workshops or certification programs.

▪ A virtual exhibit hall and sponsorship links and logos. Exhibitors can deliver their presentations in a multimedia format that can be accessed, day or night.

▪ Integration of Web conferencing tools such as LiveMeeting or Webex.

Pricing:

iCohere's Global Conference Center and Services start at $10,000 USD. Prices vary, depending on the number of participants, the length of the online conference, and the amount of consulting needed.

LearningTimes

LearningTimes designs online learning communities and produces programs and events for educational and cultural institutions, non-profit organizations, associations, and membership groups. Like The Consultants-E and iCohere, LearningTimes produces conferences that are offered completely online as well as dual-mode events. In addition, it produces online communities that support f2f conferences through online promotional events and post-conference activities. LearningTimes offers complete online conference and special event production services that encompass administrative, technical, and pedagogical factors. In addition to the services listed above, LearningTimes supplies its own expert moderators for both synchronous and asynchronous conference events.

LearningTimes has been hosting online conferences since 2002 and has been involved in the production of several large-scale conferences, including the TCC Worldwide Online Conference and the Illinois Online Conference, two of the longest-running online conferences to date. Over the last seven years, LearningTimes has utilized a wide range of technologies in order to promote these conferences, disseminate the content, and foster interaction within the conference community. They continue to provide a wide range of collaborative platforms for conference events including facilities on Squirrel Island, their property in *Second Life*. Decisions as to appropriate technologies for a given event are made in conjunction with conference organizers and presenters, with LearningTimes' staff offering their expert advice. Currently, LearningTimes online events feature capabilities for:

- ▪ Synchronous sessions for up to 1000 people using:
  - – *Event Center* by Communicast
  - – *Elluminate Live!*
  - – *Adobe Connect*
- ▪ Presentation archives
- ▪ Voice- and text-based blogging and discussion boards
- ▪ Enhanced chat tools
- ▪ Integrated instant messaging
- ▪ Online gallery talks (audio-based slide shows)
- ▪ Phone-to-Web audio messages
- ▪ Integration of third-party tools upon request

A recent example of an online professional development conference hosted by LearningTimes is the Jossey-Bass Online Teaching and Learning Conference. This conference centered around a series of books that Jossey-

Bass published on the subject of online learning. The series included a book by LearningTimes founder Jonathan Finkelstein, an internationally recognized expert on interactive online learning and community building. The conference and pre-conference workshops took place over the course of three days in October, 2008 and 2009, and attracted over 1,000 participants each year. Live orientation sessions were provided during the pre-conference so that participants could familiarize themselves with the platform and interact prior to the presentations. The conference featured live presentations spread across the three days. These live presentations were archived and available from the conference Web site to participants who were unable to attend. In addition, a live "Online Happy Hour" took place at the close of the first official day of the conference. The conference site also incorporated many areas where participants could communicate with presenters and other participants, including discussion forums, audio blogs, searchable member directories, integrated "who's on now" messaging, and special "show and tell" areas. The site with the presentation recordings remains open to conference participants long after the event is over. The cost for the 2009 conference was $269 USD and included three books from the Jossey-Bass online learning series. The cost of the pre-conference workshops was an additional $129 USD.

Pricing

LearningTimes does not provide a price structure. Each conference is negotiated independently with the client. Costs depend upon the size of the conference, number of presenters, platforms utilized, and the market.

ON24 and Unisfair

Unlike the companies described above, ON24 and Unisfair have directed their attention at the corporate sector. In addition to supporting professional development and training, these companies provide a virtual conferencing platform and services for the purpose of online trade shows, corporate communications, job fairs, and demand generation. Their clients include Fortune 500 companies from a wide variety of industries, including telecommunications, life sciences, and publishing. The CPE conference requirements of these clients are often directed toward sales and management training. This type of continuing education may take place in a dedicated conference or as part of a sales conference or product launch. These online conferences may be very large and include participants from around the globe. In addition to sales and management training, both of these companies have had experience providing continuing medical education (CME) conferences for CME providers and pharmaceutical companies. Participation in these types of events may be used for accreditation.

Both ON24 and Unisfair offer comprehensive support and services; however, the needs of their clients differ from those of higher education institutions and professional organizations. For example, corporate clients rarely require a call for papers. Presenters are usually solicited and paid well for their time. In addition, the configuration of the site is extremely important to companies who wish to include extensive branding and create an environment that reflects the corporate image. Finally, corporations require extensive site security, analytics, and reporting. These businesses are very concerned with who registers in the conference, where they go on the site, and what interactions they have. All of this information and more is gathered, analyzed, and reported on by ON24 and Unisfair.

The conferencing platforms provided by ON24 and Unisfair are very similar in appearance but differ in the features offered. Both utilize *Adobe Flash* to create a conference platform that resembles a true-to-life convention center, and both rely on webcasting technology to deliver online presentations. When participants log in to the site, they enter a grand entranceway branded by the conference sponsors and are given the option of navigating to an auditorium, exhibition hall, lounge, or resource center. The entire site can be customized for various looks. Conference hosts can choose from predesigned templates or request a custom design. The various rooms serve the following functions:

- The Conference Hall/Auditorium: This is where participants go to view conference sessions. These sessions may be live or recorded. Recorded sessions may be made available on demand for a price.
- The Lounge/Communication Center: This area is designed to promote interaction and networking between participants through live text chats and discussion forums. The features included differ between the two platforms.
- Exhibition Hall: This area may be used by exhibitors and sponsors to display information and/or products at a customized booth. Exhibitors may convey information at their booth using video, posted documents, and Web links. Communication between participants and booth representatives may take place via live text chat or a contact request via email.
- Resource Center: This area serves as a central repository for artifacts related to the conference. These artifacts may be documents, multi-media files, and Web links.

Although the platforms allow for live presentations with various features, both ON24 and Unisfair favor a webcasting presentation format. In this format, presentations are prepared in advance and recorded. The most common practice is to produce an audio poster session, whereby audio is recorded and synchronized with a PowerPoint presentation. The recorded presentation is streamed during a scheduled live session in which the presenter is in attendance. While viewing the presentation, attendees may submit questions to the presenter via a text messaging tool built into the interface. The presenter can then use streamed audio to address these questions at the end of the recorded presentation.

Although the lounge area is dedicated to interaction between presenters and participants, networking is promoted throughout the site. A search feature allows users to find other conference participants with specific profile criteria. In this way, delegates can find other individuals with similar interests or experiences, and personal messages may be sent.

Pricing

Prices for the On24 and Unisfair conference environment start in the $25K to $30K USD range for a typical three- to six-day conference. Like all other commercial platforms, the price increases with the amount of support and services required.

Conclusion

This chapter provides a glimpse of some of the commercial services that are available to conference organizers who wish to host a professional conference online but lack the necessary software, skills, and experience. The companies described here have forged the way in this new and expanding field of online conference support. However, the field is not limited to these, and we expect that as the demand for online professional conferences grows, so too will the list of service providers and the types of support that they offer. Unfortunately, finding these companies is not as easy as one would think. A Web search of related terms may turn up thousands of unrelated hits. Consequently, we do not recommend this approach. Instead, we encourage conference organizers venturing into this new arena to participate in as many online conferences as possible, noting the services that are provided by commercial companies. We also encourage those starting out to contact conference organizers for advice. Contact information can usually be found in conference promotional materials and on the conference Web site. In the course of our research, we contacted dozens of online conference organizers, looking to benefit from their experiences. Most were eager to discuss what they had learned with us. They were firm believers in the opportunities available through online conferencing and eager to expand the field by sharing what they had learned. It was through our communications with conference organizers that we learned of many of the companies described above and the services that they provided.

TABLE 7.1 Companies Offering Comprehensive Online Conferencing Services

Company Name	URL
Consultants-e	http://www.theconsultants-e.com/index.asp
Direct Learn	http://www.online-conference.net/index.htm
iCohere	http://www.icohere.com/
LearningTimes	http://www.learningtimes.net/index.shtml
ON24	http://www.on24.com/
Unisfair	http://www.unisfair.com/

8

Organizer Perspectives

Introduction

In any emerging field of practice, gathering insights and knowledge from experience is often the most effective way to learn. To collect knowledge of current activities and best practices, we sought out and interviewed over a dozen online conference organizers. These conference organizers were selected because of their experience planning, coordinating, and facilitating multiple online conferences over several years. The conferences produced by the interviewees varied in length, number of presentations, media, and organization. Some were offered free of charge, while others charged individual registration fees as high as $350 USD. Some of the smaller, more focused conferences were put together very quickly and possessed a casual atmosphere. Others were large-scale conferences covering a wide spectrum of topics. Despite the variation in the type of conference, many commonalities and issues appeared. In this chapter, we pull together some of the common themes that emerged from the interviews in order to shed light on the lessons learned and current practices of experienced online conference organizers.

Online Conferences: Professional Development for a Networked Era, pages 101–120
Copyright © 2010 by Information Age Publishing
All rights of reproduction in any form reserved.

Interview Method

The online conference organizers chosen for interviews were selected following a review of online conferences that took place between 2004 and 2009. Using Google search, a list of over 70 online conferences was created. From this list, a stratified sample of twenty exemplar conferences was selected. Indications that a conference was exemplary included the following:

- The conference ran for several consecutive years.
- The conference attracted a large audience.
- Participant feedback on the conference (found in blogs, testimonials, and evaluations) was positive.
- The conference provided opportunity for interaction between and amongst participants and presenters.

In addition to the above criteria, we attempted to select online conferences representing a variety of professional disciplines. However, we found that a large portion of online continuing professional education (CPE) conferences were organized by educational technology and IT experts. Not surprisingly, these professionals are leading the way in using these technologies to expand and improve their own professional development.

Organizers of the selected conferences were contacted by email to request a telephone interview. Representatives of commercial enterprises that had assisted in the organization of exemplar conferences by providing both the platform and the know-how were also contacted. Once consent was attained, a time for the interview was established and conference organizers were given the option of using *Skype* or their phone line for the purpose of the interview. The interviewer called at the agreed-upon time using *Skype* and recorded the call using *PowerGramo*, a *Skype* recorder. The interviews lasted from 30 to 60 minutes and followed an interview schedule as detailed next.

The Interview Questions

An interview guide was prepared in advance with the following ten questions:

1. Could you please begin by setting the context and describing the online conference that you organized? Please tell us about your primary motivations for the organization of this event.
2. What was the level of participation in the online conference as far as numbers of participants and presenters? If this online confer-

ence has been held for more than one year, please describe how the level of participation has changed over the years.

3. What types of activities were organized to support promotion, dissemination, interaction, and networking during the virtual conference?

4. Please describe the technical format of the virtual conference. What technologies were employed before, during, and after the conference?

5. What were the costs of the conference to the organizers, presenters, and participants? From your perspective, was the virtual conference a profitable event?

6. Was the conference formally evaluated? Were the results of the evaluation made public? Can we obtain them? How important is a formal evaluation to your experience of the virtual conference?

7. What do you believe are the greatest benefits of virtual conferences to presenters and participants?

8. As an organizer, what are your perceptions of the greatest value of this format of professional development?

9. What do you believe are the greatest barriers or problems associated with virtual conferences to presenters and participants? As an organizer, what are your perceptions of the challenges of this format?

10. What recommendations or best practices can you suggest to increase satisfaction and efficacy of virtual conferences? If this virtual conference has been held for more than one year, please describe any improvements that you have you implemented over the years.

Analysis & Synthesis

Transcripts of the interviews were analyzed for common and emergent themes related to the advantages and disadvantages of online CPE conferences, lessons learned, and best practices. Many of the common themes were directly related to the interview questions, such as how promotion of the online conference was best achieved. However, other themes emerged spontaneously in the interviews. For example, several of the conference organizers initiated the topic of sponsorship. A description of each of these themes and suggestions for conference organizers follows.

Common Themes from Experienced Online Conference Organizers

Choosing the Platform and Technologies

The online conferences discussed in the interviews used a wide variety of platforms and software, including both commercial and open-source. Some of the organizations also used software that they had developed themselves. Despite the variety in the technologies used, the conference organizers described similar factors influencing their choice of applications:

- Accessibility
- Simplicity
- Configurability

In regards to accessibility, conference organizers stated that they chose applications that did not require multiple downloads, were cross-platform (Mac and Windows) compatible, and were accessible to lower bandwidth users. In addition, some conferences had to provide accessibility to audiences with specific needs. For example, one of the conferences was directed toward deaf people and the professionals that work with them. Accessibility for this audience required communication technology that relied on vision as opposed to hearing.

Several conference organizers described the need for a simple and user-friendly platform. Organizers thought that if participants had difficulty navigating the conference Web site, downloading papers or recordings, or taking part in presentations or forums, it was likely that the experience would cause frustration and discourage further participation. As one interviewee said, "We don't expect that professionals will want to learn the software that delivers the platform. They want it to be easy and intuitive."

One conference organizer discussed the dilemma faced when choosing a survey tool and a wiki. The organizers of the conference had already decided to use *Moodle* as the platform for the conference. *Moodle* includes both a quiz tool and a wiki that were suitable for their purpose. However, they felt there were better tools available: "We had discussions around this, trying to decide if we should use a more robust tool for wikis [and surveys] but decided it was too much for people to start creating passwords everywhere. So we really took advantage of only the tools in *Moodle*."

An additional factor emerged from the discussions with commercial providers of conference services and software: configurability. All described the importance of providing a platform that could be configured to meet the needs of their clients. Highly configurable platforms allowed organizations to brand the site, choose the features to be included, and provided a choice of interface language.

Commercial Sponsors

Many of the online conferences studied were delivered with the assistance of sponsors. These sponsors supported the online conferences by providing conferencing platforms, content expertise, technical support, and/or financial assistance. In some cases, sponsors were integral to the organization of the conference. We witnessed several online conferences, hosted by non-profit organizations, which obtained sponsorship from commercial providers of online conferencing software and services. These commercial providers supplied not only the platform for the conference, but also provided consultation services for the organization, delivery, and evaluation of the conference.

In exchange for sponsorship, most online conferences provided advertising space, usually in the form of a logo that was linked to the sponsor's home page. Some of the online conferences went a step further and (like typical face-to-face [f2f] conferences) provided exhibition halls where sponsors could set up virtual booths. These booths provided links to the company Web site, downloadable information on the company and its products, scheduled or spontaneous live chat with a representative, and contact information. Finally, one of the conferences scheduled live vendor presentations for its sponsors using second-generation Web conferencing platforms.

Promoting the Online Conference

Email and mailing lists were, by a wide margin, the most commonly used tool to promote conference activity. These mailing lists belonged to the host organizations, sponsors, and affiliates, or postings were made to lists frequented by target participants. Some of the conference organizers offered their affiliates reduced registration fees in return for promoting the conference to their members. In most cases, a simple written invitation or announcement with conference details was emailed to the listservs. A few of the organizers added multimedia content to their promotional emails in the format of an e-card (see http://en.wikipedia.org/wiki/E-card). These multi-media invitations incorporated audio or video to attract participants to the conference. Recipients of emailed invitations were usually encouraged to forward these on to colleagues, thereby increasing the distribution.

Most of the conference organizers also stated that advertisements for the conference were posted on Web sites and in newsletters belonging to the host organizations, sponsors, and affiliates. The advertisements usually consisted of text linking to the conference Web site, but a few organizations utilized multimedia advertisements on the Web sites. Some of the organizers also posted their conference details on Web sites that advertise conferences. Two such Web sites are listed here as references: Confabb (http://www.confabb.com/) and Conference Alerts (http://www.conferencealerts.com/index.htm).

Several of the conference organizers discussed how the viral nature of the Web and social software assisted in promotion of their online conference. For example, news of online conferences was often spread through the blogosphere. When an online conference was mentioned in a blog, that information automatically went out to anyone having an RSS feed to that blog or an email alert set for information on that particular subject. In addition, news of conferences was spread through discussion in social software such as *Facebook*, *LinkedIn*, and *Twitter*. In some cases, conference organizers intentionally utilized their own or affiliated blogs and social software groups to promote their online conferences. Thus, the viral nature of the Web and Web 2.0 technologies were used to increase the number of people who were made aware of an online conference beyond the initial mailing lists.

Some of the conference organizers stated that they coordinated pre-conference events and activities in order to raise awareness of their online conferences. Events often included one or two presentations on a related topic and/or workshops. One conference published a short white paper on the subject prior to the conference. The paper was posted to the host's Web site as a discussion draft using *Comment Press*. This software allowed people to attach comments to individual paragraphs of the paper. The organizers believe that these activities generate interest and attract new participants to the conference. Pre-conference events also served to stimulate interest and help presenters gain a sense of the context and the nature of the participants. Finally, some organizers used pre-conference events to stimulate interest in an upcoming call for papers or presentations.

Call for Papers/Presentations

Like traditional conferences, the online conferences usually put out a call for papers/presentations well in advance of the conference start date. This action serves to solicit presenters but also has a secondary function of promoting the conference to potential attendees and sponsors. This was primarily accomplished using email in a manner similar to the promotion of the conference described above. Some of the online conferences used a peer review process to filter through the submitted papers. Several years ago, in an attempt to attract presenters from four-year campuses, one of the conferences began to referee and publish the conference proceedings. The organizer explained,

> Faculty are pressured to publish, and unless we can count it as a refereed publication, it's nice to do, but it's not going to help us get tenured or promoted. So I advised [the conference organizers] to create a way to have conference proceedings that are refereed so that it counts more than a regular paper presentation. So we started three years ago and we now have refereed proceedings.

Accepted authors are asked to present, and the papers are published in conference proceedings. The presentation of the paper takes on different formats, depending upon the culture and normal practices of various professional and academic communities. In some cases it is quite acceptable to read a prepared text, while often it is more common to present the paper using PowerPoint slides, increasingly augmented with links to audio and video excerpts.

Other online conferences take a much less formal approach than peer review, either inviting prospective speakers or accepting proposals based on abstracts and fit to the conference theme for presentations. None of the organizers we interviewed used automated systems to solicit, review, and select presenters. However, such submitted systems are becoming increasingly powerful and used in most large f2f conferences. In particular, the *Open Conference System* (http://pkp.sfu.ca/ocs/) from the Public Knowledge project at Simon Fraser University provides a robust open-source suite of tools to manage and schedule conference presentations.

Flexibility Afforded Conference Organizers

Organizers of online conferences often noted the flexibility and spontaneity that the online environment afforded not only participants, but also the conference organizers. Two of the conference organizers stated that they were able to pull their conferences together with minimal organization within a few months.

> I wanted to experiment with a large-scale online conference that was minimally organized, that treats the keynote speakers not as the focus of the event, but as conduits to ongoing conversations....

It seemed insane to try to pull a conference together so quickly, but we had a good idea of what we wanted to do.... I would say that if we were trying to organize something face-to-face in the same time frame, it just wouldn't have happened. Obviously, you wouldn't have time to get the word out for people to make travel arrangements and everything.

Admittedly, these were smaller conferences with fewer than ten invited presenters. However, one managed to attract well over 1,300 participants, while the other, which was much narrower in topic and geographical relevance, registered over 200 participants. In both cases, *Moodle* was used for the conference platform and live sessions were hosted on *Elluminate Live.*

Several of the conference organizers also stated that they were easily able to make last minute additions to the conference programs.

One of the virtues of an online activity is that you don't have to have all of your content lined up 4 weeks ahead of time. It can be right up to the moment. Many years, I'll get someone the first day of the conference who will say, "Hey, I've got some stuff that I'd like to show," and because of the wonders of the Web and email, I can do that. I can change the Web site to reflect that. I can send out email announcements to tell people this is happening and, boom, in the span of a couple of hours the conference has added another content item.

We had a lot of self organization. We had people who would say, "Hey I'd like to take a group out into a *Second Life* tour," and so we had about 30–40 people show up on a *Second Life* event which wasn't part of the intended proceedings, but because it was open and there were channels of communication that we tried to foster, a lot of innovative activities emerged.

Early in the conference someone brought up a suggestion from the audience through the back channel about opening up a wiki so that people could contribute notes. We did that on the fly. People took notes and put URLs into that wiki.

Spontaneous events and emergent events were reported frequently by organizers of Web-related conferences where both the organizers and participants were very comfortable with the technology. As the public becomes more at ease with Web technologies, this affordance of online conferences will likely see wider use and greater appreciation.

Participation: The Unknown Factor

Participation in an online event is much more difficult to define and determine than in an f2f event. In an f2f conference, participation is synonymous with attendance. However, in an online conference the term *par-*

ticipation is much more ambiguous. Participation is not directly related to registered numbers. When the interviewees were asked, "What was the level of participation in the online conference as far as numbers of participants and presenters?," all of the conference organizers were able to provide approximate registration numbers for the events that they had coordinated, varying from 200 participants to well over 1,000, and from 5 presenters to over 400. However, many of the organizers pointed out that the number of registered participants was not necessarily indicative of the number of people who participated in and/or benefitted from the conference. Several of these organizers stated that the number of participants that actually "showed up" or logged in to the conference Web site was much lower than the number of participants registered. However, other conference organizers felt that the number of participants that took part in the conference was much greater than the registration numbers indicated.

There were several reasons given for this ambiguity. First, because the cost of attending an online conference is relatively inexpensive, it is more likely that registered attendants might drop out of the conference entirely if personal or professional time conflicts arise. The reduced cost of attending an online conference also makes it easier for registrants to justify attending only a few presentations that are of particular interest to them. On the flip side, it is also easier for people to attend online conferences unseen. For example, a group may log in using a single password and attend a live session that is broadcast at a central location. In addition, two or more people can utilize a single log-in to gain access to the conference Web site. To further confuse the issue, some conferences are open to public viewing without or with optional formal registration. However, usually only registered participants are permitted to attend live presentations and interact. However, anyone can lurk, view recordings, and obtain information from the conference Web site without registering. These hidden participants are not included in the registration numbers, but enjoy many of the benefits offered by the conferences.

Participation in an online conference is also difficult to track, as it may take place outside of the conference platform. Many conference Web sites enable registered participants to subscribe to forums. New postings are then "pushed out" via email, making it possible for participants to read and respond to them outside of the conference site. Participants may also receive new postings via RSS or *Twitter* and respond to these postings on their own blogs rather than in the conference forum. As one conference organizer stated, "It is possible to follow along without ever having to open the Web page."

Finally, participation in an online conference is difficult to define, as it takes many different forms. For example, a registered participant may choose to view presentation recordings and never be seen or listed as a participant in a live session. Several of the conference organizers pointed out that the number of people listening to and watching the recorded presentations after the event far outstripped the number of participants that attended the live session. Participants may also choose to lurk in forums and never post. These people are not participating in an observable manner; nevertheless, they are on the conference Web site and benefitting from the information there. In addition, the dichotomy between presenter and participant in an online conference is somewhat blurred. Two of the conference organizers explained that presenters at their conferences were charged reduced registration fees, as they were also considered participants. The presenters were able to take part in all of the conference events, they received copies of published materials, and they had access to all information on the conference Web site.

The uncertainty over participation numbers is an important issue to address for several reasons. The first and most obvious reason is the potential loss of revenue. Although many online conferences are offered free of charge, others do require a registration fee to cover costs. Depending on the format of the online conference, the platform used, and the support required, the costs to conference organizers may be substantial. Reimbursement for these expenses may be diminished by groups who purchase a single registration and broadcast the event at a central location. In addition, sponsorship for an online conference may be difficult to gain if registration numbers are viewed as too low or attendance from particular sectors is not visible. Finally, knowing the number and extent of participation is a minimal requirement for calculating the return on investment for either a sponsor of participants or the conference organizers.

The conference organizers addressed the ambiguity of participation and registration in a variety of ways. Some stated that by charging a small registration fee, they hoped to gain commitment to the conference while, at the same time, not discouraging registration. Some offered group rates to educational institutions and sponsor organizations. By doing so, they were able to better track registration and participation, and they were at least partially recompensed. In order to address the issue of participation outside of the conference parameters, several of the conferences used conference tags in order to identify content appearing outside of the conference parameters. This content was aggregated using *Pageflakes* or *Hitchhikr* and linked to the conference site. In this way, outside participation and content was still archived and accessible from the conference Web site.

Despite the uncertainty that arose over the concept of participation, one consistency appeared. All of the organizers whose conferences had been held for successive years reported increased registration over the years. In addition, the dispersion of attendees had increased, with more countries represented each year. One conference organizer attributed the rising registration numbers to peoples' increasing familiarity with online environments and collaborative platforms. Whatever the reason, it is clear that online conferences are growing in popularity.

Making the Delegates Comfortable and Encouraging Interaction

Many of the conference organizers discussed the importance of first making the participants feel comfortable with the conference platform and with each other. The feeling was that if participants were comfortable they would be more likely to interact. Consequently, many of the conference organizers stated that their first priority was to familiarize participants with the conference environment and with each other so that they would be ready and willing to participate fully in the conference on day one. This was accomplished in a variety of ways.

First, many of the organizers opened the conference Web site prior to the actual conference start date. They informed delegates via email how to log in and how to access help, if necessary. Once logged in, participants were often provided further information and guidance. Some of the conference Web sites included an embedded welcome video, while others provided tips on how to participate effectively in an online conference. In some cases, pre-recorded presentations and papers were made available for viewing a week prior to the conference start date so that participants would be prepared to enter into the related discussion forums as soon as they were opened. In almost every case, delegates were encouraged to explore the site and complete a personal profile, including pictures, biographical information, and contact information. The profiles served to enable networking throughout the conference and afterwards. More recently, conference platforms are embedding social networking tools that allow delegates to find others with similar interests, "befriend" one another, schedule times for synchronous gatherings, "wheel and deal," and otherwise network with each other.

Many of the online conferences opened with introductions and icebreaker activities. These activities often took place prior to the actual conference start date. Many of the online conferences opened with an introduction forum or live reception. These forums and sessions allowed participants to interact with the technology and with each other prior to the formal proceedings. Several of the conferences tried to incorporate fun and creative introductions. These conferences included galleries where delegates were encouraged to post "mug shots" (a picture of the delegate with his or her favorite mug) or "window shots" (a picture of something outside of his or her office or home window), webcams, street views or maps of their location, links to favorite resources, et cetera. The photos/maps and other media were accompanied by a brief explanation and/or introduction. Some of the conferences that included sessions in *Second Life* also asked participants to post pictures of their avatars in an avatar gallery so that they would be recognized when they were "in world." In addition to the profiles and galleries, several of the conference Web sites utilized social map applications such as *Frappr* maps or *Attendr* maps. These online maps allowed conference participants to add their names, photos, and messages directly on the Web page embedded with the map. Not only did these maps provide another means of becoming more familiar with other participants, but they provided a quick visual of the geographical dispersion of the participants. The idea behind many of these activities is to build a "conference community where people begin to recognize each other."

Finally, as mentioned above, some of the conferences hosted pre-conference events and orientations. These events not only served to attract participants to the conference, they also provided an opportunity for conference participants to familiarize themselves with the platform, the content, and each other. As one conference organizer stated, "in the pre-conference, everybody gets fired up about the conference and everybody makes sure that they have the technology that they need and [makes] sure that they can get into the conference community. We start the process of networking and we avoid people getting lost on the first day." These events took place anywhere from weeks to days prior to the actual conference.

Promoting Attendance and Participation during the Conference

In order to keep participants current during the conference, many of the organizers posted daily bulletins reminding participants of the events that would be taking place that day. These bulletins were usually posted to the conference site and often pushed out via email to the conference participants. However, one of the conference organizers stated that they were moving to SMS text messaging for this purpose. Finally, some of the conferences asked their session moderators to remind participants of other activities coming up throughout the day. "This is done at the closing of the sessions to keep people engaged and aware of things coming up."

Live Presentations

In discussing the format and technologies used for presentations, all of the organizers interviewed stated that their conferences have, over the past few years, turned more and more to second-generation live conferencing technology. The platforms most commonly used allowed presenters to interact with the audience using Voice over Internet Protocol (VoIP) voice interaction while displaying PowerPoint slides. Beyond the obvious fact that synchronous conferencing technologies are now more accessible, the conference organizers gave several reasons for this move to second-generation technologies:

- Excellent sound quality even for lower bandwidth users
- Greater social presence
- Ease of use for both presenters and participants
- The option to use text messaging
- Additional features such as video, breakout rooms, whiteboards, and application sharing
- Adaptability and accessibility for blind and deaf audience members

Another reason, heard repeatedly, for using live conferencing platforms, including *Second Life*, was the ability to record the presentations and archive them on the conference site. Recordings could also be converted to mp3 formats so that users had the choice of listening to a podcast or watching the entire presentation with the visuals. Many of the organizers stated that the live presentations were followed by asynchronous discussion forums related to the presentation, so participants unable to attend the live session could still view the recorded presentation and take part in the asynchronous discussion. Finally, many of the online conferences, even those charging a registration fee, made the recordings freely available to the public when the conference closed.

> We had tremendous uptake in people listening to it, much more than listen to it live. Even months after the fact we still had instances where over 1,100 users per month would listen to one podcast or one presentation from the event. So the recordings far, far outstripped the live attendance.

Supporting Presenters

All of the conference organizers, with one exception, stressed the importance of supporting the presenters, particularly when using live platforms. Many recommended orientation sessions with an experienced moderator prior to the presentation. These orientations allowed the moderators to uncover and mitigate any technical issues and gave the presenters an opportunity to become familiar with the presentation platform. Many of the organizers stated that they encouraged the presenters to interact with the audience and instructed them on how to incorporate the tools (especially audience polls, text chat, etc.) that these platforms provide for this purpose. It is very easy in a Web conference to present simple polls with instant results displayed. This helps generate a level of audience participation that is usually not available even in f2f sessions. Some of the organizers also gave the presenters access to the live presentation rooms so that they could rehearse whenever they wanted to on their own. Finally, all of the conference organizers stated that it was important to have an experienced moderator present during the actual presentation. The responsibilities of the moderator were described as:

- Introductions
- Operating the recording tool during the presentation
- Technical assistance for participants and presenter
- Facilitating the discussion
- Monitoring the text chat and helping the presenter prioritize questions and responses
- Closing the presentation
- Reminding participants of upcoming events and evaluation opportunities

Commercial providers of online conferencing services also stated that, when necessary, they helped presenters prepare pre-recorded presentations. These were usually converted to *Adobe Flash*, as most conference participants had the software necessary to view *Flash* presentations.

Presenter Freedom to Choose Media

Some of the conferences did not allow for any variety in the mode of presentation. They used a single technology for all presentations and a uniform presentation format. For example, one of the conferences studied delivered all presentations using the Web conferencing system *iVocalize*. This software "provided superb audio even over low speed internet connections, the ability to display PowerPoint presentations, and cross-platform compatibility." In addition, the conferencing system allowed for an unlimited number of participants. Audience members were able to communicate with the presenter using the audio capabilities or text messaging. Presentations were recorded and available for viewing on the conference site. Each presentation followed the same pattern: live, voice annotated PowerPoint presentation followed by questions and discussion. Although this single for-mat may be seen as limiting, it should be noted that this was an extremely large global conference, with approximately 400 presentations from over 80 countries. Many of the presenters and participants were new to online conferencing and did not have high bandwidth connectivity. Another of the conferences presented a unique situation in that a large portion of its audience was deaf. Consequently, many of the presentations in this confer-ence were simply papers posted on the site, followed by text format discus-sion forums. These examples demonstrate the need for organizers to con-textualize the technology and the conference activities to meet the need of target participants.

Other conferences, particularly those serving professionals comfort-able with IT, allowed for greater variety in the technologies and formats used for presentations. Rather than dictating a particular format or mode of presentation, some of the conference organizers offered presenters a choice of presentation media and assisted them with selecting a technology that best suited the subject of the presentation and the audience. In other cases, the presenters were given complete freedom in choosing their mode of delivery, provided that the technology could be used effectively, given the size of the audience and bandwidth restrictions. One conference organizer stated that he exerted "no editorial control" over the tools that presenters used to deliver their content. He simply established a conference Web site that was set up as a portal directing participants to the various presentations. The technologies used varied widely. "Some of it was proprietary, [software] that they have created themselves. Some of them have used *Skype* in the past; some of them have used *WebEx* in the past. Some people have used asynchronous Web discussion tools." According to the conference Web site, presenters had also used various desktop sharing software, podcasts, and open-source software such as *DimDim*.

The freedom of choice given to presenters seemed to fall along a con-tinuum between the extremes of "no choice" and "total freedom to choose." Factors that influenced the position on the continuum were:

- Presenter comfort with the technology
- Capacity and accessibility of tools within the conference delivery platform
- Participant comfort
- Presentation topic
- Accessibility
- Size of the audience
- Ease of use

Encouraging Interaction and Networking (Building a Community)

Interaction and networking are critical components of online CPE conferences. Conference organizers stated repeatedly that they tried to encourage interaction within the formal events, stating that without interaction the event would offer little more than a paper or broadcast. Many also promoted the type of interaction that occurs at live conferences in the hallways and lounges after the formal events are over. They supported professional networking in the hopes of building an online community of practice that would persist after the conference had ended. Conference organizers listed several methods used to support both formal and informal interaction.

Promotion of Interaction Within Formal Events

The most common interaction design was the use of discussion facilitators/moderators during both live presentations and asynchronous discussions. Moderators were usually chosen because they were familiar with the subject and comfortable with the environment. Some were volunteers, while others were paid for their services. Paid moderators were used most commonly when a commercial provider was commissioned to help organize the online conference. In many cases, moderators were trained prior to the conference. Moderators of live presentations often worked with the presenters prior to the presentation, helping them become comfortable with the software and encouraging them to build interaction into the session.

> We've been trying to work with our presenters as we go along, especially presenting in [*Second Life*]—trying to move to as much audience participation as possible, because there's almost no reason to be in [*Second Life*] to watch someone talk over slides. One of our [presenters] actually performed a musical mashup performance which broke out into some spontaneous dance and discussion....

During live presentations, moderators continue to encourage interaction by asking questions and stimulating discussion. In addition, moderators are often asked to monitor the text chat so that questions and comments that are posted there are included in the discussion.

The promotion of interaction in asynchronous discussion boards presents unique challenges to conference organizers and forum moderators. Some of the attributes of this medium also pose complications. For example, an asynchronous discussion board is open 24/7 for postings. This allows delegates to participate at a time convenient to them; however, it also means that participants may fall behind in discussions very quickly. In busy forums, with hundreds of postings, delegates may become overwhelmed and give up on participating entirely. During the interviews, two sugges-tions for alleviating this problem were made. The first was the use of forum software with push technology using either email and/or RSS. This tech-nology enables participants to subscribe to a discussion forum of interest. Whenever a post was made to the forum, subscribers would receive an email notification of the new posting or notification of the posting would appear in their RSS reader. Subscribers could also choose to receive notification only when a response to one of their own postings was made or to a discus-sion thread that they selected as having particular interest or relevance. In this way, subscribers were less likely to fall behind in a discussion forum. However, one of the conference organizers interviewed provided a caution about the use of email push technology. During one of the online confer-ences that he helped to organize, the subscription default had been set so that participants would receive an email notification of every posting. Par-ticipants became distressed when they received hundreds of emails regard-ing each new posting in all of the various conference forums. Consequently, he recommended establishing the forum settings such that email push-out occurs only at the request of the participant.

A second method used to alleviate the problem of falling behind in discussion forums was daily summaries, which could be distributed as a posting in the forum or as an email. One of the conference organizers, realizing that the forums were very active both day and night, decided to provide daily summaries. This helped the participants to stay up-to-speed on what was being said, but it required a moderator very familiar with the subject area.

Promotion of Informal Interaction and Professional Networking

Acknowledging the importance of the interaction that occurs between and after presentations in f2f conferences, many of the conference orga-nizers attempted to create social areas within the conference environment where this type of discussion might occur. The software used for these so-cial areas varied greatly. Some conferences used asynchronous discussion forums, some used live conferencing platforms, and others used immersive platforms such as *Second Life*. In all cases, participants were invited to drop in and chat with whoever was present. Conferences using live interactive software also scheduled social hours. Participants were invited to attend these informal events that took place at various times throughout the con-ference. Receptions in *Second Life* often included music and dancing.

In addition to the social areas, most of the conference platforms also encouraged one-to-one networking using the participant profiles. The con-ference profiles enabled delegates to contact each other using the conference's instant messaging feature, email, *Skype*, or telephone, depending on which contact method a participant had chosen to list/enable in their profile. Most of the conference platforms included a search feature that allowed delegates to search for other participants according to a given characteristic. This enabled participants to connect with others who possessed similar interests or backgrounds. The feature worked in much the same way as *LinkedIn*, a popular social software used to connect professionals.

Finally, most of the conference platforms studied included a resource area where participants could share related content, links, or other information about their own work. In the resource area, participants could embed links and download documents or multimedia files, thereby creating a dynamic, practice-based repository of shared professional knowledge and experiences.

Promotion of Interaction Outside of the Conference Platform

As the use of more sophisticated Web social software has grown, conference organizers have taken advantage of these platforms for the purpose of promoting "back channel" interaction. Many conferences now have *Facebook* groups, a *Twitter* site, or dedicated bloggers. Other conferences have established conference tags for their participants to use when posting comments or conference-related content outside of the conference platform. These postings can then be easily found and linked to the conference site using *Technorati*, *Pageflakes*, or *Hitchhikr*.

> The expectation wasn't that people contribute to the conference in our terms and in our space, but rather that people were able to contribute to the event exactly as they wanted. So, if they had an existing blog, there was no reason for them to now contribute to our blog, or our *Moodle* site.... We realized in advance that people have a different sense of familiarity with participating in decentralized environments.

Dealing with a Global Audience

One of the advantages commonly attributed to online conferences is that they can be attended from anywhere in the world, thus enabling the sharing of experiences and perspectives between members of a global audience. However, the dispersion of the participants can also present challenges for conference organizers. For example, the opportunity to interact must be somewhat convenient for participants from a variety of time zones. The online conference organizers interviewed presented a variety of methods to address this issue.

Live events present the greatest barrier to global participation, as they require all participants to attend simultaneously. Many conference organizers have addressed this issue by recording the live presentations and then posting them to the conference Web site as soon as possible. This makes the recording accessible to participants not able to attend, but it does not allow them to converse with the presenter and/or other participants on the subject. Consequently, many of the conferences studied also hosted an asynchronous discussion forum related to each live presentation. The forums enabled participants to discuss the content and share their own experiences. Presenters were often part of the discussion, but not always.

A second method for addressing the issue of time zones was demonstrated by the largest online conference in the study. The size of this conference and the number of presentations enabled the organizers to offer live sessions 24/7. In 2008, 382 live presentations ran sequentially for 10 full days, day and night. The presenters, who represented over 80 countries, were able to choose a time slot that was convenient for them, while delegates from around the world were able to participate at any time. In addition, the conference organizers recorded all of the sessions and posted these to the conference Web site immediately following the live presentation.

Another complication posed by a global audience is the language barrier. This issue is addressed in much the same way online as it is in f2f conferences. That is, through the help of technological and human interpreters. Many of the commercial conferencing platforms examined in this study offer a multi-language user interface. Participants can, independently, choose from a given selection the language they wish to use on the conference Web site. Although none of the conferences included in this study used human interpreters, the commercial providers that were interviewed stated that they had, in the past, provided human interpreters at an additional cost to clients when necessary. They stated that the request for interpreters was most common when providing online conference services to global corporations, as these organizations have both the need and the financial resources to support this additional expense.

Perceived Benefits of Online Conferences

When conference organizers were asked to describe the benefits or greatest perceived value from this format of professional development, their answers were strikingly similar. Most felt that online conferences excelled over f2f because of the availability of content and peer interaction before, during, and after the conference. Many of the conferences opened the Web site early to registered participants. They allowed the participants to proceed with introductions and to view static content such as papers and webcasts prior to the formal start date. In addition, the conference Web sites were open 24/7. Thus, delegates could access the content and post to asynchronous discussions at any hour. Finally, all of the online conferences studied remained open long after the formal conference dates had passed so that participants could go back to view recordings, look up conference related content, or access contact information for other participants.

Many organizers also noted the cost reductions associated with online conferences for both participants and organizers. Finally, they appreciated the flexibility of the medium for scheduling, expanding, or contracting events and activities

Conclusion

This chapter described in detail the themes that emerged from interviews with online conference organizers. Their experiences and insights provided valuable information leading to a better understanding of how to produce an effective online CPE conference. In the final chapter, we draw from these themes and from the literature in order to provide an outline of best practices for those organizing an online conference.

9

Summary of Best Practices and Making Change Happen

Change is hard because people overestimate the value of what they have—
and underestimate the value of what they may gain by giving that up.
—James Belasco and Ralph Stayer, *Flight of the Buffalo* (1994)

The greatest danger in times of turbulence is not the turbulence;
it is to act with yesterday's logic.
—Peter Drucker

Introduction

The interviews with conference organizers, our study of the academic research literature, and our own participation in online conferences have demonstrated the value and unfolding potential of this form of continuing professional education (CPE). However, we also recognize that the all-important technical and social context within which these events occur is in flux. Communications technologies continue to become more accessible,

Online Conferences: Professional Development for a Networked Era, pages 121–130

121

more functional, and more affordable. The economic and environmental costs of travel continue to increase. The need for individuals and organizations to function at high levels of efficiency and effectiveness increases. Thus, the stage is set for an escalation in the number and variety of online conferences.

Traditional conference organizers wishing to ride this tide of change may benefit greatly from the experiences of those who have broken ground in online professional conferences. And so, in this final chapter, we offer a summary of the common themes and best practices that emerged from our study. In addition, recognizing that the change to online conferences may be difficult to implement, we close this chapter with a brief examination of models of organizational change and provide suggestions on how the change to online conferencing may be encouraged and facilitated within organizations that are reticent.

Summary of Best Practices

In times of change such as these, it is challenging and occasionally unproductive to spend too much time trying to determine what works best in all contexts. Nonetheless, the interviews with the online conference organizers revealed many strategies and activities associated with the successful design and delivery of an online CPE conference. Some of these were unique to a given conference, while other strategies seemed to work well across many contexts. These latter strategies are summarized and included here.

1. Choose software that is easily accessible, simple to use, and configurable. The software must be appropriate to both the objectives of the conference/presentation and the needs of the audience.
2. When promoting the online conference, take advantage of the viral affordances of the Web by asking email recipients to forward their invitations to colleagues and friends. Web 2.0 applications such as blogs, *Twitter*, and social networks are also used effectively for this purpose.
3. Cultivate partnerships and find sponsors that can provide content expertise, technical assistance, and/or financial support to the conference. Sponsors also help by promoting the conference to members of their own organizations and associates. Scheduling opportunities for sponsors to participate in the conference as presenters allows them an opportunity to focus audience attention on their product and allows interested participants opportunity to learn from relevant vendors and service providers

4. When soliciting presenters, make it worth their while by offering some or all of the following:
   - Access to all of the conference content
   - Stipend or honorarium. The amount of these payments can be considerably less than requested for face-to-face (f2f) conference presentations, as time and travel savings are as attractive to presenters as they are to the participants.
   - Refereed and published proceedings. Publication of proceedings is a critical attractor for presentations by academics and is generally useful to all participants, as it provides a persistent link to relevant materials. The use of Web-based content management systems, where documents in multiple formats (e.g., PowerPoint, Word, PDF) can be stored and distributed simplifies this task. The use of *Google Docs*, *Slideshare*, and other free services makes this type of distribution very cost effective for conference organizers.
   - An opportunity to share research interests and get feedback from peers around the globe in a highly interactive environment. A conference "tag" and a conference *Twitter* feed allows participants to provide both immediate and time-delayed opportunity to reflect on presentations, provide feedback to presenters, and share insights—all valuable promotion and feedback for quality presenters.
   - Exposure and promotion. Make sure that online abstracts, biographies, and affiliations of presenters and summaries are posted on the open Net so that they will be retrieved and indexed by Web search engines.
5. In order to track registration numbers and participation in both free and paid conferences:
   - Require all participants to register prior to participating in the conference. However, ensure that the conference Web site contains a privacy policy listing what uses (if any) will be made of information provided by registrants.
   - Require participants to use a log-in to access the conference Web site, but of course provide provision for lost passwords or forgotten login names.
   - Offer group rates to potentially large participant and sponsor organizations.
6. Make participants feel comfortable in the environment by:
   - Opening the site early for exploration

- Including information on the conference home page to orientate and guide delegates.
- Incorporating activities and applications that help delegates build familiarity with the platform and each other:
  - Introduction forum
  - Profile page
  - Picture gallery
  - Ice-breaker activities
  - Social maps (e.g., *Frappr* maps)
  - Live pre- and post-conference social events and orientations

7. Encourage participation by sending out daily reminders of upcoming events via email, SMS, *Twitter*, and/or RSS. Also remind people of upcoming events at the end of live presentations.

8. Create a conference tag to identify and aggregate conference-related content that gets posted outside of the conference platform.

9. Take advantage of the knowledge possessed and suggested by participants and the flexibility afforded by the technology in order to add to and improve the online conference. In many cases, improvements can be made very quickly. It may not be necessary wait to until the next conference to implement changes and improvements.

10. Provide temporal flexibility by:
    - Using second- and third-generation software services that can record and archive activities and be presented from the conference site.
    - Creating asynchronous discussion forums that are associated with live presentations or conference themes so that participants can interact at a time that is convenient to them.
    - Scheduling live presentations at various times throughout the day and night in order to accommodate time zone shifts if a world audience is expected. If a localized audience is expected, scheduling consistency (e.g., keynotes at 10:00 AM) helps establish a consistent flow to the conference.

11. Employ facilitators/moderators who are experienced with the software and the content. This may require more than one moderator per presentation. Moderators serve several purposes:
    - Schedule a training, time synchronization, and technical check-in session for presenters a few days before the scheduled event

- Assist the presenter during live presentations by helping load and access audiovisual materials and adjust sound levels appropriately
- Moderate live presentations
- Record live presentations
- Mitigate technical difficulties
- Facilitate interaction and questions during synchronous and/or asynchronous sessions

12. In order to avoid participants becoming overwhelmed in asynchronous forums:
    - Use platforms that have email push technology, RSS, and *Twitter* feeds that can be controlled by the participant.
    - Provide daily summaries and daily aggregation services for email for those who choose digest versions of email interactions.

13. In order to promote social interaction and networking between participants:
    - Create social spaces within or linked directly to the conference platform where participants can meet just to chat using both text and voice.
    - Schedule live social events in second-generation (live Web conferencing) and third-generation (immersive technologies such as *Second Life*) platforms.
    - Enable and encourage participants to post contact and interest information on searchable profile pages.
    - Use a platform that enables instant messaging, *Twitter*, and participant search features.

14. Include a resource area where presenters and participants can post conference-related materials such as documents, multimedia files, and links.

15. Allow access to the conference Web site for at least 12 months after the conference officially closes.

Finally, as a result of our research into evaluation (Chapter 6), we encourage online conference organizers to resist the temptation to simply evaluate participant reactions using online questionnaires immediately following the event. The online environment offers new opportunities for evaluation and provides systems to ease the collection and dissemination of evaluation data. Organizers should give careful consideration to these affordances when deciding on the evaluation approach to be used.

Making Change Happen

Moving an organization or profession from a culture and practice of f2f conferences to one blended with online conferencing requires careful and effective change management. Change is never easy and, too often, attempts at changing complex systems and established behaviors are not successful. Fortunately, the organizational and educational literature offers useful theories and models to help innovators instigate and guide this necessary change process. In this chapter we overview some of these models and provide suggestions for effectively developing the motivation and actions necessary to take advantage of online conferencing.

Online conferences are an innovation and, as such, require energy and effort to successfully implement within any organization. The noted Harvard academic Clayton Christensen (1997) in his study of technological innovation usefully differentiates between sustaining and disruptive technologies. Sustaining technologies allow individuals or organizations to do what they are already doing, but in ways that are incrementally more effective or more efficient. In an f2f conference context, one can think of the sustaining value of computers and networks to generate and distribute promotional items, register participants, create delegate surveys, and distribute program updates. Such sustaining innovation allows users to communicate with more ease and power and allows organizers to more cost effectively promote and evaluate their programs. These sustaining innovations do not disrupt the normal timing, scheduling, and other responsibilities of organizers and participants, nor do they disrupt the basic economic model upon which the conference is based.

Distributive technologies, by contrast, either very dramatically change the function or the business model under which a system or organization functions. The online conference radically changes the organizer's role from one of booking venues and hotels, scheduling meeting rooms, hosting f2f sessions, and handing out evaluation forms to one that focuses on promotion, online coordination, recording, and online evaluation of conference activities. Disruptive technologies are often led by low-end priorities. A service that was once expensive and exclusive now becomes available to whole new groups of users. Ironically, this opening of the market may not be attractive to suppliers or even consumers of the existing services who have become accustomed to the level of service (with associated costs and profits) of higher-end products. However, often the quality of the low-end product improves dramatically and quickly rises, causing demand for the high-end service to evaporate. As an example, one can consider the reduction in consumer experience of those watching the first black-and-white television programs as compared to that experienced at a live theatre or the cinema. As televisions improved in color, contrast, and size, the difference in quality decreased, creating a much larger market for televised programming as compared to either the live theatre or the movie theatre market.

There is little doubt that the development of online conferences is a low-end and disruptive innovation. The online conference opens access to professional development at an economic and ecological cost that is far less than that associated with f2f conferences. As predicted, the experience is not as rich for participants and the profit potential much reduced for organizers. Yet, as we have seen through the three generations of online conferences (Chapter 2) and the case studies in this book, the experience for participants continues to improve. We can expect both trends towards increased users and improvements in quality and capacity, thereby creating ongoing disruption to traditional f2f conferences. However, describing an innovation (disruptive or sustaining) as inevitable does little to enhance our capacity to create a future within which we most want to participate. Thus, the next section talks of ways to encourage and support the development of disruptive innovations such as online conferences.

Supporting and Championing Innovation

So far in this text we have focused upon what we consider to be compelling (though disruptive) advantages of online conferences as compared to or to enhance f2f conferences. However, change and innovation management is a very complicated process, and rarely are innovations adopted or disregarded based solely on costs or perceived advantages. Rather, innovation adoption takes place in the messy world of real people engaged in political and social interactions with each other and with the systems and other organizations they have created. Before moving to concrete action plans for effective innovation management, it is useful to overview these social and political factors.

The German writer William Kruger has created an iceberg model of change management (Figure 9.1) that nicely illustrates the forces at work in any innovation adoption process. In the model, residing in the visible area above the surface is the familiar triangle of *cost*, *quality*, and *time* that comes to mind immediately when thinking about change in any organization or in our personal lives. Obviously, there must be cost savings, realistic time requirements, and acceptable quality outputs if an innovation is to be adopted. However, focusing exclusively on these factors without considering the social and organizational factors hidden beneath the surface is unlikely to lead to innovation adoption.

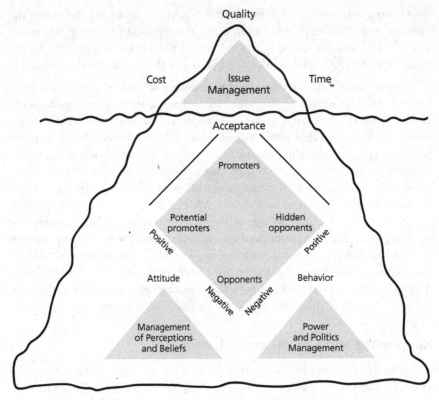

Figure 9.1 W. Kruger's (1996) iceberg model of change management.

The first level below the surface is populated by those decision makers and potential participants who are likely to be both in favor of and thus promoters of the innovation and those overtly or secretly opposed to the innovation. Online conferences, because of their cost effectiveness, can expect support from cost-conscious managers and from participants who are, by reason of geography or other commitments, bound to specific locations. Alternatively, those more socially inclined managers and participants who view the opportunity to temporarily escape from home and office life through travel will likely be opposed to online conference participation. Although much has been written about the digital divide between those who are comfortable and regularly use technology and those who do not, evidence is growing that such gaps are narrowing as technology and skill of use become ubiquitous in most areas of professional and recreational life. Further, talk of Net generations and huge divides between older and younger users are also falling away as older adults increasingly embrace technology for a variety of personal and professional uses. Indeed, there is likely to be more variation within demographic groups as both individual affinity and rejection of technology begin to become more apparent than any demographic variations. Obviously, meeting and communicating with both promoters and opponents is useful, but one is more likely to find support from the early adopters and innovators who tend to be promoters and supporters of technology-based innovation.

Perhaps of greatest influence and interest are the deep issues related to management, power, and politics that ground the base of the iceberg. Face-to-face conferences are deeply embedded into the custom and practice of many professions. These scheduled events have become important networking opportunities and, as mentioned earlier, often serve as perks of membership or employment within the profession. Thus, efforts to change should be focused on enhancing and extending rather than eliminating these events. In addition, compelling opportunities to meet and network online should be developed in every online conference. Many influential power brokers are little exposed to networking innovations, and thus attention should be set to provide means by which managers can experience firsthand participation in online events. Finally, inviting influential decision makers to have active roles in speaking to and participating in online conferences allows them opportunity to be promoters rather than opponents.

From this theoretical background we now move to the more practical steps of change management suggested for champions of online conferencing.

1. Promote both the ecological and the cost savings provided to both delegates and sponsors of professional development activities. In times of economic recession, curtailment of professional development activities and travel restrictions are common. These cutbacks provide opportunity to introduce the radical cost savings possible through online conferences.

2. Expose f2f conference delegates to distributed learning technologies by facilitating participation of external participants. There are many ways in which social networking technologies such as *Twitter*, blogs, and webcasting can be used in conjunction with conferences. Highlighting and encouraging delegates to participate in these activities will allow them to benefit from both the online and the f2f learning. Once exposed to the online possibilities, they will be more likely to support completely online conferences.

3. Gather and distribute testimonials and survey data from online conference delegates. Online conferencing provides benefits to delegates that many may find hard to understand until they read

of the new opportunities afforded to those who cannot attend f2f conferences.

4. Have at least one key note presenter participate from a distance using large screen videoconferencing in each and every f2f conference. This exposure forces delegates to experience for themselves the engagement possible through videoconference delivery by a remote speaker.

5. Ensure that online conferences or introductory seminars contain a blend of asynchronous and synchronous activities. Synchronous activities bring enhanced presence and immediacy to the conference. Asynchronous interaction allows for reflective response and demonstrates the capacity of learning that is time-shifted and thus most accessible.

6. Capture and record segments of the conference and obtain permission to distribute these "nuggets" widely to expose dispersed audiences to the power of online conferences.

7. Calculate and disseminate the ecological costs associated with f2f conferences by calculating the atmospheric carbon generated by business travel. A very high percentage of business travel is associated with attendance at professional development events or trade shows. These ecological costs can be greatly reduced by reducing f2f and increasing online conferencing.

8. Create backup plans highlighting online activities for events that must be cancelled due to pandemics or natural catastrophes. Be ready for the opportunities provided by crisis.

Conclusion

Throughout this book, we described the multiple benefits of online professional conferences and listed the many catalysts of change that are affecting the evolution toward online CPE conferences. However, we would not argue that the f2f conference will entirely disappear, just as movies did not render the live theatre obsolete, nor has television destroyed the movie theater. Rather, consumers and organizers will learn to participate using both older models and new innovations, creating innovative blends of online and f2f experiences that meet the diverse and changing needs of high-end and the increasingly large number of low-end participants.

References

2008 industry report: Gauges and drivers (2008). *Training, 45*(9), 16–34.

American Evaluation Association. (2004). The American evaluation association guiding principles for evaluators. Retrieved January 25, 2010 from http://www.eval.org/GPTraining/GP%20Training%20Final/gp.package.pdf

Anderson, L. & Anderson, T. (2009). Online professional development conferences: An effective, economical and eco-friendly option. *Canadian Journal of Learning and Technology 35*(2). Retrieved June 1, 2010, from http://www.cjlt.ca/index.php/cjlt/article/view/521

Anderson, L., & McCarthy, K. (2006). Text-based conferencing: Features vs. functionality. *The International Review of Research in Open and Distance Learning* [Online] *6*(3). Available from http://www.irrodl.org/index.php/irrodl/article/view/272

Anderson, T. (2005). Online education innovation: Going boldly where others fear to thread. In G. Kearsley (Ed.). *Online Learning: Personal reflections on the transformation of education.* (pp 1–11). Englewood Cliffs: Education Technology Publications.

Anderson, T. (1996). The virtual conference: Extending professional education in cyberspace. *International Journal of Educational Telecommunications, 2*(2/3), 121–135.

Anderson, T., & Christiansen, J. (2004). Online conferences for professional development. In C. Vrasidas & G. V. Glass (Eds.), *Online Professional Development for Teachers* (pp. 13–30). Information Age Publishing.

Anderson, T., & Kanuka, H. (1997). On-line forums: New platforms for professional development and group collaboration. *Journal of Computer Mediated Communication, 3*(3). Retrieved from http://jcmc.indiana.edu/vol3/issue3/anderson.html

Online Conferences: Professional Development for a Networked Era, pages 131–140

Anderson, T., & Mason, R. (1993). The Bangkok project: New tool for professional development. *American Journal of Distance Education, 7*(2), 5–18.

Association Trends (May 16, 2008). Interested in replicating the Social Responsibility Summit? Retrieved July 3, 2008 from http://www.icohere.com/2008AssociationTrends.pdf

Axtell, C. M., & Maitlis, S. (1997). Predicting immediate and longer-term transfer of training. *Personnel Review, 26*, 201–213.

Azzaretto, J. F. (1990) Power, responsibility and accountability in continuing professional education. In R. M. Cervero and J. F. Azzaretto & Associates (Eds.) *Visions for the future of continuing professional education* (pp. 25–50). Athens: The University of Georgia Center for Continuing Education.

Bailenson, J., Blascovich, J., Beall, A. C., & Loomis, J. M. (2003). Interpersonal distance in immersive virtual environments. *Personality and Social Psychology Bulletin, 29*, 1–15. Retrieved May 28, 2009, from http://www.recveb.ucsb.edu/pdfs/BailensonBlascovichBeallLoomis-02.pdf

Barriball, L. K. & While, A. E. (1996). Participation in continuing professional education in nursing: findings of an interview study. *Journal of Advanced Nursing, 23*, 999–1007.

Belanger, E., & Jordan, D. H. (2000). *Evaluation and implementation of distance learning: Technologies, tools and techniques.* Hershey, PA: Idea Group Publishing.

Berge, Z. L. (1999). Interaction in post-secondary web-based learning. *Educational Technology, 39*(1), 5–11.

Bernthal, P. R. (1995). Evaluation that goes the distance. *Training and Development 49*(9), pp. 41–45.

Brennan, B. (1990). Continuing professional education: Promise and performance. *Australian Education Review, 30*, 154.

Bronack, S., Sanders, R., Cheney, A., Riedl, R., Tashner, J., & Matzen, N. (2008). Presence pedagogy: Teaching and learning in a 3D virtual immersive world. *International Journal of Teaching and Learning in Higher Education, 20*(1), 59–69.

Brown, J. S., & Duguid, P. (2000). *The social life of information.* Boston: Harvard Business School Press.

Burge, E. (1994). Learning in computer conferenced contexts: The learners' perspective. *Journal of Distance Education, 9*(1), 19–43.

CDIAC (Carbon Dioxide Information Analysis Centre). (2010). *Global CO_2 emissions from fossil-fuel burning, cement manufacture, and gas flaring: 1751–2007.* Oak Ridge, Tenessee: Boden, T. & Marland, G. Retrieved July 15, 2010, from http://cdiac.ornl.gov/ftp/ndp030/global.1751_2007.ems

Cervero, R. (1985). Continuing professional education and behavioural change: A model for research and evaluation. *The Journal of Continuing Education in Nursing, 16*(3), pp. 85–88.

Cervero, R. (1988). *Effective continuing education for professionals.* San Francisco: Jossey-Bass.

Cervero, R. M. (1992). Professional practice, learning, and continuing education: An integrated perspective. *International Journal of Lifelong Education, 11*(2), 91–101.

Cervero, R. (2001). Continuing professional education in transition, 1981–2000. *International Journal of Lifelong Education, 20*(1), 16–30.

Cervero, R. M., Azzaretto, J. F., & Associates (Eds.) (1990) *Visions for the future of continuing professional education.* Athens, Georgia: The University of Georgia Center for Continuing Education.

Chapman, D., Wiessner, C., Storberg-Walker, J. & Hatcher, T. (2007). New learning: A different way of approaching conference evaluation. *Knowledge Management Research & Practice, 5,* pp. 261–270.

Childress, M., & Braswell, R. (2006). Using massively multiplayer online role-playing games for online learning. *Distance Education,* 27(2), 187–196. Retrieved October 23, 2007 from http://0-web.ebscohost.com.aupac. lib.athabascau.ca/ehost/pdf?vid=14&hid=115&sid=597b07d0-0ce4-4fbd-964a-2e43a4e84176%40sessionmgr102

Choi, M. (2006). Communities of practice: An alternative model for knowledge creation. *British Journal of Educational Technology, 37*(1), 143–146.

Christensen, C. (1997). *The innovator's dilemma: When new technologies cause great firms to fail.* Cambridge: Harvard University Press.

Cross, J., O'Driscoll, T., & Trondsen, E. (2007). Another life: Virtual worlds as tools for learning. *eLearn Magazine.* Retrieved May 28, 2009 from http://www.elearnmag.org/subpage.cfm?article=44-1&section=articles

Curran, V. R., Fleet, L., & Kirby, F. (2006). Factors influencing rural health care professionals' access to continuing professional education. *Australian Journal of Rural Health, 14*(2), 51–55.

Daley, B. J. (2000). Learning in professional practice. *New Directions for Adult and Continuing Education, 86,* 33–42.

Daley, B. J. (2001). Learning and professional practice: A study of four professions. *Adult Education Quarterly, 52,* 39–55.

Daley, B. J. (2002). Continuing professional education: Creating the future. *Adult Learning, 13*(4), 15–17.

Darby, L. E. (2009). Franchise development series recap: "Unconference" format successful, '09 session planned. *Franchising World 41*(2), pp. 79–80.

Day, M. (1996). Pedagogies in virtual spaces: Writing classes in the MOO. *Kairos: A Journal for Teachers of Writing in Webbed Environments, 1*(2). Retrieved October 8, 2007 from http://kairos.technorhetoric.net/1.2/coverweb/coverweb.html

Dennis, P. (2004). California's experience with distance education for adult basic learners. *Adult Basic Education, 14*(3), 135–152.

Dublin, S.S. (1990). Maintaining competence through updating: Understanding the challenge facing today's professionals. In S. L. Willis and S. S. Dublin (Eds.), *Maintaining Professional Competence* (pp. 1–7). San Francisco: Jossey-Bass.

Dolezalek, H. (2003). Collaborating in cyberspace. *Training,* 40(4), 32–37.

Eastin, M., & LaRose, R. (2000). Internet self-efficacy and the psychology of the digital divide. *Journal of Computer Mediated Communications, 6*(1). Retrieved January 19, 2004 from http://jcmc.indiana.edu/vol6/issue1/eastin.html

Fernandez, K. (2007). The ultimate roundtable. *Associations Now 3*(12), 55–60. Retrieved January 27, 2010 from http://www.asaecenter.org/Publications Resources/ANowDetail.cfm?ItemNumber=28995

Fitzpatrick, J. L., Sanders, J. R., & Worthen, B. R. (2004). *Program evaluation: Alternative approaches and practical guidelines* (third edition). Boston, MA: Pearson Education Inc.

Freidson, E. (1983). The theory of professions. In R. Dingwall & P. Lewis (Eds.), *The Sociology of Professions* (19–47). New York: St. Martin's Press.

Furze, G. & Pearcey, P. (1999). Continuing Education in nursing: A review of the literature. *Journal of Advanced Nursing, 29*(2), 355–363.

Goodyear, P., & Steeples, C. (1999). Asynchronous multimedia conferencing in continuing professional development: Issues in the representation of practice through user-created videoclips. *Distance Education, 20*(1), 31–48.

Google. (2009). *About Google Wave.* Retrieved June 10, 2009 from http://wave.google.com/about.html

Hansen, J. E. (2006) October 17). Can we still avoid dangerous human-made climate change? *Social Research: An International Quarterly of Social Sciences*, pp. 949–974.

Harasim, L., Hiltz, S. R., Teles, L., & Turoff, M. (1995). *Learning Networks.* Cambridge, MA: MIT Press.

Heckman, R., & Annabi, H. (2003). A content analytic comparison of FTF and ALN case-study discussions. *Proceedings of the 36th Hawaii International Conference on System Sciences.* Retrieved October 2, 2007 from http://www.aln-research.org/data_files/articles/full_text/heckman03.pdf

Herring, S. (1999). Interactional coherence in CMC. *Journal of Computer-Mediated Communication, 4*(4). Retrieved October 8, 2007 from http://jcmc.indiana.edu/vol4/issue4/herring.html

Hew, K. F., & Cheung, W. S. (2003). An exploratory study on the use of asynchronous online discussion in hypermedia design. *E-journal of Instructional Science and Technology, 6*(1). Retrieved October 18, 2007 from http://www.usq.edu.au/electpub/e-jist/docs/Vol6_No1/pdf/Hew_%20Final.pdf

Hiltz, S. R. (1994) *The virtual classroom: Learning without limits via computer networks.* Norwood: Ablex Publishing Corporation.

Houle, C. O. (1980) *Continuing Learning in the Professions.* San Francisco: Jossey-Bass.

Hron, A., & Friedrich, H. F. (2003). A review of web-based collaborative learning: Factors beyond technology. *Journal of Computer Assisted Learning, 19*, 70–79.

Hurteau, M., & Nadeau, M. (1985). The pros and cons of responsive evaluation. (ERIC Document Reproduction Service No. ED 267 103).

IAPCO. (2009). Annual survey 2006–2008. Retrieved Oct. 1, 2009 from http://www.iapco.org/survey_of_members_activities.cfm?page_id=117

ICCA. (2009). Association Day 2009 evaluation. News and publications web page. Retrieved Oct. 1, 2009, from http://www.iccaworld.com/npps/story.cfm?nppage=1964

IPCC (2007). Summary for policymakers. In S. Solomon, D. Qin, M. Manning, Z. Chen, M. Marquis, K. B. Averyt, M. Tignor & H. L. Miller (Eds.), *Climate Change 2007: The Physical Science Basis. Contribution of Working Group I to the Fourth Assessment Report of the Intergovernmental Panel on Climate Change.* Cambridge, UK: Cambridge University Press.

Ivanoff, G. (1998). Running a virtual conference: Lessons learned. In C. McBeath and R. Atkinson (Eds.), *Planning for Progress, Partnership and Profit.* Proceedings EdTech'98. Perth: Australian Society for Educational Technology. Retrieved August 28, 2007 from http://www.ascilite.org.au/aset-archives/confs/edtech98/pubs/articles/ivanoff.html

Jacobs, N., & McFarlane, A. (2005). Conferences as learning communities: Some early lessons in using "back-channel" technologies at an academic conference: Distributed intelligence or divided attention? *Journal of Computer Assisted Learning, 21*(5), 317–329.

Jaeger, P. T., & Xie, B. (2009). Developing online community accessibility guidelines for persons with disabilities and older adults. *Journal of Disability Policy Studies 20*(1), pp. 55–63.

Jonassen, D., Davidson, M., Collins, M., Campbell, J., & Bannan Haag, B. (1998). Designing constructivist learning environments. In C. M. Reigeluth (Ed.), *Instructional Theories and Models* (Vol II, pp. 215–239). Mahwah, NJ: Lawrence Erlbaum.

Kasser, J. (2001). Enhancing conferences and symposia using web based asynchronous techniques. *The 11th International Symposium of the INCOSE, Melbourne, Australia.* Retrieved September 26, 2007 from http://www.unisa.edu.au/seec/pubs/01papers/enhancing%20webconf.pdf

Kaufman, R., Keller, J., & Watkins, R. (1995). What works and what doesn't: Evaluation beyond Kirkpatrick. *Performance and Instruction, 35*(2), pp. 8–12.

Kimura, B., & Ho, C. (2008). Online conferences and workshops: Affordable and ubiquitous learning opportunities for faculty development. *Proceeding from Distance Learning and Internet Conference 2008*, Tokyo, Japan. Retrieved March 5, 2009, from http://www.waseda.jp/DLI2008/program/proceedings/pdf/session3-1.pdf

Kirkpatrick, D. (2010). 50 years of evaluation. *Training and Development, 27*(1), p. 14.

Kirkpatrick, D. (1977). Evaluating training programs: Evidence vs. proof. *Training and Development Journal, 31*(11), pp. 9–12.

Kirkpatrick, D. (1998). *Evaluating training programs: The four levels* (second edition). San Francisco, CA: Berrett-Koehler Publishers Inc.

Kirkpatrick, J. (1996). TCC online conference chronicle. Retrieved October 17, 2007 from http://english.ttu.edu/kairos/1.2/coverweb/Kirkpatrick/index.html

Klintberg, I. G. (1976). A responsive evaluation of two programs in medical education. *Studies in Educational Evaluation, 2*(1), pp. 23–30.

Knowles, M. S. (1980). *The modern practice of adult education: From pedagogy to andragogy* (Rev. ed.). Englewood Cliffs: Prentice Hall/Cambridge.

Knox, A. B. (2000). The continuum of professional education and practice. *New Directions for Adult and Continuing Education, 86,* 13–22.

Kruger, W. (1996). Implementation: The core task of change management. *Community of European Management Schools, 1,* 77–96.

Lapadat, J. (2002). Written interaction: A Key Component in Online Learning. *Journal of Computer-Mediated Communication, 7*(4). Retrieved October 3, 2007 from http://jcmc.indiana.edu/vol7/issue4/lapadat.html

Lin, L., Cranton, P., & Bridglal, B. (2005). Psychological type and asynchronous written eialogue in adult learning. *Teachers College Record, 107*(8), 1788–1813.

Linden, T. (2009, Aug. 12). The Second Life economy—Second quarter 2009 in detail. [Second Life Blog]. Message posted to https://blogs.secondlife.com/community/features/blog/2009/08/12/the-second-life-economy—second-quarter-2009-in-detail

Livneh, S., & Livneh, H. (1999). Continuing professional education among educators: Predictors of participation in learning activities. *Adult Education Quarterly, 49*(2), 91–106.

Marsick, V. J., & Watkins, K. E. (2001). Informal and incidental learning. *New Directions for Adult and Continuing Education, 89,* 25–34.

Mathieu, J., Tannenbaum, S., & Salas, E. (1992). Influences of individual and situational characteristics on measures of training effectiveness. *Academy of Management Journal, 35,* 828–847.

McKerlich, R., & Anderson, T. (2007). Community of inquiry and learning in immersive environments. *Journal of Asynchronous Learning Networks, 11*(4). Retrieved from http://www.sloan-c.org/publications/jaln/v11n4/index.asp

Menn, J. (2009, May 25). Virtual conference victory for Cisco Systems. *The Financial Times Limited.* Retrieved May 25, 2009 from http://www.ft.com/cms/s/0/15cf7be8-494c-11de-9e19-00144feabdc0.html?nclick_check=1

Meyer, J. M. (2007). *Continuing professional education and its impact on the practices and careers of certified public accountants* (Doctoral dissertation, Louisiana State University, 2007). Electronic Thesis & Dissertation Collection. Available from http://etd.lsu.edu/docs/available/etd-04072007-160534/

Minshull, G. (2006). Evaluation report highlights: Innovating e-Learning 2006 online conference. Retrieved August 30, 2007 from http://www.jisc.ac.uk/uploaded_documents/evaluation%20highlights%20innovating%20e-learning%202006.doc

Minshull, G. (2004). *Online conferencing and staff development.* Retrieved August 30, 2007 from http://www.online-conference.net/downloads/ol_staffdev. pdf

Mott, V. W. (2000). The development of professional expertise in the workplace. *New Directions for Adult and Continuing Education, 86,* 23–31.

MPI. (2009). Facts and figures. Retrieved Sept. 30, 2009 from http://www.mpi-web.org/AboutMPI/Facts.aspx

Mungania, P., & Hatcher, T. (2004). A systemic, flexible, and multidimensional model for evaluating e-learning. *Performance Improvement, 43*(7), pp. 33–39.

Murphy, E. (2001). Investigating the multiple worlds of teaching through multiloguing. *Educational Technology & Society, 4*(3). Retrieved October 6, 2007 from http://www.ifets.info/journals/4_3/murphy.pdf

Murphy, E., & Coleman, E. (2004). Graduate students' experiences of challenges in online asynchronous discussions. *Canadian Journal of Learning and Technology, 30*(2). Retrieved October 3, 2007 from http://www.cjlt. ca/content/vol30.2/cjlt30-2_art-2.html

Nowlen, P. M. (1988) *A new approach to continuing education for business and the professions: The performance model.* New York: Macmillan.

Ortega, L. (1997). Processes and outcomes in networked classroom interaction: Defining the research agenda for L2 computer-assisted classroom discussion. *Language Learning & Technology, 1*(1), 82–93.

Parr, B. (2009). Could Google Wave redefine email and web communication? *Mashable: The social media guide.* Retrieved June 10, 2009 from http:// mashable.com/2009/05/28/google-wave/

Pena-Shaff, J., Martin, W., & Gay, G. (2001). An epistemological framework for analyzing student interactions in computer-mediated communication environments. *Journal of Interactive Learning Research, 12*(1), 41–68.

Phillips, J. (1997). *Handbook of training evaluation and measurement methods* (third edition). Houston, TX: Gulf Publishing Company.

Queeney, D. S. (2000). Continuing professional education. In A. L. Wilson and E. R. Hayes (Eds). *Handbook of Adult and Continuing Education, New Edition.* San Francisco: Jossey-Bass.

Ravn, I. (2007). The learning conference. *Journal of European Industrial Training 31*(3), 212–222.

Rossman, M. (1999). Successful online teaching using an asynchronous learner discussion forum. *Journal of Asynchronous Learning Networks, 3*(2). Retrieved October 4, 2007 from http://www.aln.org/publications/jaln/index.asp

Salmon, G. (2000). *E-moderating: The key to teaching and learning online.* Sterling, VA: Kogan Page.

Schön, D. A. (1987). *Educating the reflective practitioner.* San Francisco: Jossey-Bass.

Schwan, S., Straub, D. & Hesse, F.W. (2002) Information management and learning in computer conferences: Coping with irrelevant and unconnected messages. *Instructional Science,* 30, 4, 269–289.

Schwier, R. A., & Balbar, S. (2002). The interplay of content and community in synchronous and asynchronous communication: Virtual communication in a graduate seminar. *Canadian Journal of Learning and Technology, 28*(2). Retrieved October 11, 2007 from http://www.cjlt.ca/content/vol28.2/schwier_balbar.html

Scriven, M. (1967). The methodology of evaluation. In R.E. Stake (Ed.), *Curriculum Evaluation* (pp. 39–83). American Educational Research Association Monograph Series on Evaluation, No. 1. Chicago: Rand McNally.

Second Life. (2009). In *Wikipedia: The Free Encyclopedia* [Web site]. Retrieved June 12, 2009 from http://en.wikipedia.org/wiki/Second_life

Sgouropoulou, C., Koutoumanos, A., Goodyear, P., & Skordalakis, E. (2000). Acquiring working knowledge through asynchronous multimedia conferencing. *Educational Technology & Society, 3*(3). Retrieved September 28, 2007 from http://www.ifets.info/journals/3_3/a06.html

Shield, M., Wiesner, P., Curran, C., Stark, G., Rauch, S., Stergachis, A., & Thompson, J. (2005). The northwest's hot topics in preparedness forum: A novel distance-learning collaborative. *Journal of Public Health Management and Practice (Suppl), 11*(6), S25–32.

Shimabukuro, J. (2000). The evolving virtual conference: Implications for professional networking. *The Technology Source,* September/October. Retrieved October 29, 2009 from http://www.technologysource.org/article/evolving_virtual_conference/

Siemens, G. (2005). A learning theory for the digital age. *Instructional Technology and Distance Education, 2*(1), 3–10. Retrieved from http://www.elearnspace.org/Articles/connectivism.htm

Siemens, G., Tittenberger, P., & Anderson, T. (2008). Conference connections: Rewiring the circuit. *Educause Review,* 43(2). Retrieved from http://www.educause.edu/EDUCAUSE+Review/EDUCAUSEReviewMagazineVolume43/ConferenceConnectionsRewiringt/162675

Sierra, K. (2007). Face-to-face trumps Twitter, blogs, podcasts, video.... *Creating Passionate Users* [Web site]. Retrieved September 17, 2007 from http://headrush.typepad.com/creating_passionate_users/2007/03/sxsw_interactiv.html

SLanguages. (2009). SLanguages: The conference for language education in virtual worlds [Website]. Retrieved on April 15, 2008, from http://www.slanguages.net/home.php

Smith, C. A., Cohen-Callow, A., Dia, D. A., Bliss, D. L., Gantt, A., Cornelius, L. J., Harrington, D. (2006). Staying current in a changing profession: Evaluating perceived change resulting from continuing professional education. *Journal of Social Work Education 42*(3), 465–482.

Social Networking. (2009). In *Wikipedia: The Free Encyclopedia.* Retrieved May 21, 2009 from http://en.wikipedia.org/wiki/Main_Page

Solomon, S., Plattner, G-K., Knutti, R., & Friedlingstein, P. (2009). Irreversible climate change due to carbon dioxide emissions. *Proceedings of the*

National Academy of Sciences of the United States of America (PNAS), 106(6), 1704–1709.

Spiegel, A., Bruning, R., & Giddings, L. (1999). Using responsive evaluation to evaluate a professional conference. *American Journal of Evaluation, 20*(1), pp. 57–67.

Stake, R. (Ed.). (1975). *Evaluating the arts in education: A responsive approach.* Columbus, OH: Charles E. Merrill Publishing Co.

Stake, R. E. (1976). A theoretical statement of responsive evaluation. *Studies in Educational Evaluation 2*(1), 19–22.

Stake, R. E. (1985). Responsive evaluation. In T. Husen and T. N. Postlewaite (Eds.), *International Encyclopedia of Education* (Vol. 7, pp. 7405–7408). New York: Pergamon Press.

Stevens, V., & Dudeney, G. (2009). Online conferences and teacher professional development: SLanguages and WiAOC 2009. *Teaching English as a Second or Foreign Language 13*(1). Retrieved October 29, 2009 from http://www.tesl-ej.org/wordpress/past-issues/volume13/ej49/ej49int/?wscr=

Stohl, A. (2008). The travel-related carbon dioxide emissions of atmospheric researchers. *Atmospheric Chemistry and Physics, 8,* 6499–6504. Retrieved December 16, 2008 from http://www.atmos-chem-phys.net/8/issue21.html

Sulčič, I. (2009). *Virtual worlds in education and Moodle.* Paper presented at the 3rd International Slovenian MoodleMoot 2009. Retrieved August 10, 2009 from http://www.scribd.com/doc/15731198/Virtual-worlds-in-education-and-Moodle

Tam, M. (2000). Constructivism, instructional design, and technology: Implications for transforming distance learning. *Educational Technology & Society 3*(2), 363–373.

Taulli, T. (2007). IBM takes a conference call. *The Motley Fool.* Retrieved September 24, 2007 from http://www.fool.com/investing/general/2007/08/27/ibm-takes-a-conference-call.aspx

Totty, J. (2005). Business solutions: Making online meetings easier. *The Wall Street Journal Online.* Retrieved August, 28, 2007 from https://www.gotomeeting.com/t/afg2m/2007_Q2/Thinkofit_text/article/g2m_b3lp?Target=m/wsjArticle.tmpl&AID=10385003&PID=60261

Unconference. (2009). In *Wikipedia: The Free Encyclopedia.* Retrieved October 27, 2009 from http://en.wikipedia.org/wiki/Main_Page

Van Bruggen, J. M., Kirschner, P. A., & Jochems, W. (2002) External representation of argumentation in CSCL and the management of cognitive load. *Learning and Instruction, 12*(1), 121–138.

Wang, Y. (1999). Online conference: A participant's perspective. *THE Journal (Technological Horizons in Education), 26*(8), 70.

Warschauer, M. (1997). Computer-mediated collaborative learning: Theory and practice. *The Modern Language Journal, 81*(4), 470–481.

Web 2.0. (2009). In *Wikipedia: The Free Encyclopedia.* Retrieved May 21, 2009 from http://en.wikipedia.org/wiki/Main_Page

Wieman, A. (2001). Organising virtual conferences: Lessons and guidelines. *Research Report, No. 2.* Retrieved October 3, 2009 from http://www.iicd. org/articles/IICDnews.import1852

Wenger, E. (1999). Learning as social participation. *Knowledge Management Review, 6,* 30–33.

Wenger, E., McDermott, R. A., & Snyder, W. (2002). *Cultivating communities of practice: A guide to managing knowledge.* Boston: Harvard Business School Press.

Wenger, E., McDermott, R., & Snyder, W.M. (2002). *The wealth of knowledge: Intellectual capital and the twenty-first century organization.* New York: Doubleday.

Wiesenberg, F. & Hutton, S. (1996). Teaching a graduate program using computer-mediated conferencing software: distance education futures. *Journal of Distance Education, 11*(1), 83–100. Retrieved August 27, 2007 from http://cade.athabascau.ca/vol11.1/wiesenberg.html

Williams, C. (2002). Learning online: A review of the literature in a rapidly expanding field. *Journal of Further and Higher Education, 26*(3), 263–272.

Woolley, D. (2007). Real-time web conferencing: An independent guide to software and services enabling real-time communication. *Think of It* [Web site]. Retrieved on September 24, 2007 from http://thinkofit.com/webconf/realtime.htm